"This book is a must-read for thos⸱⸱⸱⸱⸱⸱⸱⸱⸱⸱⸱⸱⸱⸱⸱⸱⸱⸱⸱⸱⸱⸱⸱⸱⸱⸱⸱⸱⸱ f-
filiation or context. It is equally ⸱⸱⸱⸱⸱⸱⸱⸱⸱⸱⸱⸱⸱⸱⸱⸱⸱⸱⸱⸱⸱⸱⸱⸱⸱⸱⸱ r
with children, for pastors as well as ⸱⸱⸱⸱⸱ professionals who work with children in emotional
health settings. "

Trevecca Okholm, author of *Kingdom Family: Re-Envisioning God's Plan for Marriage and Family*

"Who will wrestle for the spiritual formation of a child? Who will show us how to steward the soul of a little one? Who can help us become *witnesses* instead of *instigators* for the ones we hold precious? Lacy Finn Borgo can. She's someone who has learned the ancient lesson—to not block but to bring the little children to Jesus."

Jonathan R. Bailey, cofounder of Dwell and board chair of Renovaré

"If you are a parent or grandparent or if you have ever been a child, this book is for you. Lacy Borgo writes in a way that is humorous, folksy, insightful, practical, and engaging. And she is sneaky-wise. Like her friend Jesus, she knows that if you want to find the kingdom of God, you'll need to listen well to children. They know how to receive it and have much to teach. So buy this book because you want to be a better caregiver to one or more children you know and love, but read it to deepen your own relationship with God."

Gary W. Moon, founding executive director of the Martin Institute and Dallas Willard Center, Westmont College, author of *Becoming Dallas Willard*

"There are so many things to love about *Spiritual Conversations with Children*—solid theology, spiritual insights, practical suggestions, stories of children and their relationship with God. But what I love most is Lacy's deep appreciation and love for children. She invites us to enter into the world of young people and their relationship with God—to understand what is going on in their lives and how God is at work in those lives. She introduces us to spiritual direction with children and teaches us how to build listening relationships with them and to appreciate and value their lives and faith. This book is a gift to parents, grandparents, and all those who work with children and their families."

John Roberto, author, instructor, and consultant in lifelong faith formation

"Jesus honored children with his attention and blessings. Borgo continues that legacy with this astonishing book on caring for the very real, vibrant, spiritual world of children. She inspires us to see children in a fresh way, no matter their circumstances or outward mannerisms. She teaches us to come alongside and nurture these small souls with spiritual conversations. This book is for anyone who wants to be a better adult to children as together we seek intimacy with Christ."

MaryKate Morse, mentor and author

"Borgo invites us into the sacred space of spiritual direction with children, showing us how to come alongside them on their spiritual journey. Along the way, she weaves a textured theological tapestry that is accessible and engaging, developing a trinitarian theology of generosity (versus scarcity). Her lyrical writing draws us in; her humble approach wins our hearts; her touching stories make spiritual conversations seem doable. I believe Borgo's work will be another children's spirituality classic, deeply moving, tender, affective—a book for the ages."

Holly Allen, chair of the Children's Spirituality Summit, professor of family studies and Christian ministries, Lipscomb University

"Lacy Borgo has written a wonderful book. If you can get through it without shedding tears, your heart has turned to stone. Lacy understands children, the ways of the Holy Spirit, and God's special love for these precious, developing image-bearers. This book will help those whose vocation involves working with children, and all those who remember—and still experience—the goodness and difficulty of growing up. A wise and wonderful book."

Chris Hall, president of Renovaré

"Through her obvious respect for those children with whom she companions, her own sacred curiosity in their everyday experiences, and her personal confidence in God's hidden presence in their lives, Lacy also shows how we can *be* with those children in our midst. Her message is gently insistent: children are God's image bearers. God is personally present and lovingly active in their lives. Be attentive and listen well. This book is a special gift for all those grandparents, parents, pastors, teachers, and therapists who want to interact creatively with children around their spiritual formation."

Trevor Hudson, lecturer at Renovaré and the Fuller Seminary DMin program in spiritual direction, author of *Discovering Our Spiritual Identity*

"Read this book and you'll get all you need from a master teacher: a foundation of child development insights, intriguing street-level techniques for connecting with kids, verbatim sessions, and ideas for addressing hot-button issues. Also excellent for parents and grandparents, aunts and uncles."

Jan Johnson, spiritual director, author of *Meeting God in Scripture*

"This book is a gift to the next generation of friends of children. We have needed to listen to the spiritual life of children for a long time and Lacy has taught us how. In *Spiritual Conversations with Children*, Lacy shares her bag of tricks, helping us learn to be present with a child. Illustrated with well-chosen stories, this book is a reminder of Jesus' presence with ordinary little people. Yet it is also an introduction to a new worldview of children's ministries, the view from a child's own encounter with God."

Evan Howard, professor of Christian spirituality at Fuller Theological Seminary and author of *Praying the Scriptures*

"In this book Borgo opens our eyes to the many ways we can engage with children, providing a variety of tools and resources that can be utilized to engage children in their spiritual relationship with God that are founded on an understanding of children and their developmental needs. She also reminds us of our posture, a posture of listening, encouraging, and receiving when working with children."

Mimi Larson, guest assistant professor of Christian formation and ministry, Wheaton College

"Knowing Lacy, I had suspected that reading *Spiritual Conversations with Children* would forever change the way I interact with my kids, and it has. But what I didn't anticipate is the way this book has ministered deeply to the child who still lives in me—helping me to begin to recognize movements of God in my younger life that I had previously missed. If there are children in your life—or if you ever were a child—this book has much to offer."

Carolyn Arends, recording artist, author, and Renovaré director of education

SPIRITUAL
CONVERSATIONS
WITH CHILDREN

LISTENING TO GOD TOGETHER

LACY FINN BORGO

An imprint of InterVarsity Press
Downers Grove, Illinois

InterVarsity Press
P.O. Box 1400, Downers Grove, IL 60515-1426
ivpress.com
email@ivpress.com

*InterVarsity Press® is the book-publishing division of InterVarsity Christian Fellowship/USA®, a movement of students
and faculty active on campus at hundreds of universities, colleges, and schools of nursing in the United States of
America, and a member movement of the International Fellowship of Evangelical Students. For information about
local and regional activities, visit intervarsity.org.*

*While any stories in this book are true, some names and identifying information may have been changed to protect the
privacy of individuals.*

Cover design and image composite: Cindy Kiple
Interior design: Cindy Kiple
Cover image: mother and daughter painting: © Archv / iStock / Getty Images Plus
All interior images are by Lacy Finn Borgo. Used with permission.

ISBN 978-0-8308-4669-6 (print)
ISBN 978-0-8308-4833-1 (digital)

Printed in the United States of America ∞

*InterVarsity Press is committed to ecological stewardship and to the conservation of natural resources in all our
operations. This book was printed using sustainably sourced paper.*

Library of Congress Cataloging-in-Publication Data
A catalog record for this book is available from the Library of Congress.

P 25 24 23 22 21 20 19 18 17 16 15 14 13 12 11 10 9 8 7 6 5 4 3 2 1
Y 41 40 39 38 37 36 35 34 33 32 31 30 29 28 27 26 25 24 23 22 21 20

CONTENTS

For the children at Haven House

LEARNING FROM CHRISTOPHER

Reality [is] what you run into when you are wrong.

DALLAS WILLARD

ARMED WITH A MASTER'S DEGREE in education and accolades for leading educational workshops for the New York State Teacher's Union, I had no reason to question my firmly held knowledge on the growth and development of children. In my very young mind and heart I thought I knew all there was to know about childhood. Reality, a gift of grace, came knocking when Christopher walked into my fourth-grade classroom.[1] It was only week two of the school year and he had already been shuffled from classroom to classroom and suspended from school altogether. I was the third and last fourth-grade teacher to welcome him into her classroom. One more incident and he would have to go to the alternative school for children with behavioral disorders.

Christopher was a smart kid, using whatever power he possessed for his survival. In my classroom the situation was no different.

Within the first week he jumped out of the second-story window and shimmied down the fire escape to avoid a math test. Strangely enough, the break for both Christopher and me came when he was suspended from the cafeteria. His disruptive behavior had become an over-whelming obstacle for getting lunch served to eight hundred children. The lunch staff had no choice but to ban him from the cafeteria.

I had run into reality. I had no more knowledge to draw upon and the system had run out of beneficial options. In the beginning it was simply a matter of location. Christopher could not be in the cafeteria, so he ate lunch with me in our classroom. As lunch was my only break of the day, I had no desire to teach, lecture, or even change him. Over the course of our seven months of lunches, however, I began to become curious. Christopher talked all through our lunches. He would recount bits of his days or tell me stories about his family. Sometimes he would reflect on the deeper things in his life, like how he felt about his mother leaving, why he thought death was so scary, and the unbelievable kindness of our vice principal, Mr. Bell. I began to wonder what was going on inside of Christopher. Christopher had astonishing hope in the future and in the goodness of people; he possessed a mystery that I could not define or control.

As a Christ-follower I wondered what ways God was reaching for Christopher in all the mess. To preserve the public school sepa-ration of religious talk from academics, I began to ask Christopher about goodness rather than about God. What did goodness look like to him? When did something good happen to him? What was it like to experience goodness? At the time I knew little about the three great transcendental ideas: goodness, truth, and beauty.

However, I knew that God was good and where goodness was, God was there too.

Inspired by my curious inquiry, Christopher opened up his inner world to me. There was more to Christopher than what was presented in his behavior, more going on in him than the school counselors could deduce. During our lunches I gave him no lectures, I taught him nothing. In fact, I spoke very little besides asking a few questions. Christopher made it through the fourth grade and even the fifth. He went off to middle school, but sometimes he would return to my classroom and hang around after class, longing to be listened to.[2]

Christopher taught me how to listen. My time with him started a nearly thirty-year exploration into understanding the spiritual lives of children. This journey has yielded new insights, fresh understanding, deep empathy, and, most surprisingly, healing for my own childhood wounds. It is my hope that you will gain some of the treasures I have. This book presents what doctoral research and experience have taught me about having spiritual conversations with children. I began listening to God with children in 2014 at Haven House. Haven House is a transitional facility for homeless families. It is dorm-style living for homeless families that includes a two-year program designed to help move them into sustainable independence. I meet with children one-on-one as a spiritual companion to them. We call it "holy listening," taken from Margaret Guenther's book on spiritual direction.

In this book we will explore how spiritual conversations with children support their life with God. We will learn not only what makes these conversations unique but also how to have them. We will begin by learning from Jesus. Jesus had a hospitable and welcoming posture toward children. We will uncover the role of longing, belonging, and connection in a child's life with God. Diving into spiritual formation with children as a guide for spiritual growth, we will think deeply about the four elements of children's spiritual formation and the implications for children and the adults who long to accompany them. We will take a look at three Ps—*posture, power,* and *patterns*—and how each of these shape spiritual conversations with children. We will notice the natural power dynamic between adults and children and how Jesus used his body to empower and honor children.

Pushing against our natural inclination to talk at or teach children, we will learn how our eyes and ears help us to contemplatively listen to children, and further how this listening opens a child to respond to God's invitation. We will learn from children how play and projection help them to experience God and reflect upon their life in light of that experience. As we become more fluent in play and projection, we will learn how to help children recognize the Spirit's movement in their life and respond to this movement in a way that is unique to their natural inclinations.

Finally, we will rest in mystery. The human relationship with divine love is to be lived not dissected. Our grasp of the workings of this relationship is at best a generous guide; at worst it is a mechanized jail cell. When we accompany a child on their journey with God, we do so from the position of knowing only in part. We hold this pearl of great price and marvel with wonder at its beauty.

Learning to be a listening adult to children yields enduring benefits. When children have a listening companion who hears, acknowledges, and encourages their early experiences with God, it creates a spiritual footprint that will shape the way a child engages with God, others, and themselves. Spiritual conversations with children foster resiliency in the life of the child. Children who have learned to listen to their inner life and orient that life in divine community have a calibrated inner compass that can guide them when the storms of life inevitably come.

Parents are essential listening companions, and children need additional adults who are present to listen and to encourage them in their life with God. A child's life with God suffers spiritual anemia when there is a lack of community. You can be one of the listening adults who supports a child's spiritual life.

Spiritual conversation with children also benefits the adult doing the listening. When we are fully present and open to another, we will be changed. Our own childhood self will be offered the invitation to connect with God. The Spirit longs to heal old wounds and to embrace long-buried gifts. Indeed, as you listen to God with a child, the child will lead you into a fuller experience of God's love and acceptance.

If you are a parent or grandparent, this book is for you. Listening to a child's journey with God is a sacred gift we can give them. Family is the most deeply formational social context we will ever live in. If you are a pastor, friend, or teacher of children, this book is for you. To accompany children in their life with God has the potential to shape the classroom, the congregation, and the world. If you are a spiritual director, this book is for you. It is my hope that it will offer a few guides and a heap of courage for you to begin to host listening spaces for children. These young beloveds of God are participants in the present and future; to invest in them is to witness the unfolding of grace.

one

LEARNING
FROM JESUS

Let the little children come to me; do not stop them; for it is to such as these that the kingdom of God belongs. Truly I tell you, whoever does not receive the kingdom of God as a little child will never enter it.

JESUS

I LIVE ON A SMALL HOBBY FARM in Western Colorado. We have horses, chickens, dogs, cats, and goats. After twelve years of keeping company with goats, I've learned a thing or two. For example, I have learned that if a fence won't hold water it won't hold a goat. I have learned that horses, dogs, and goats can read human body language and will use this superpower in the service of their belly.

After a few years into our little goat adventure, I also learned that when a mama goat is getting ready to have her kids, she prepares. "Kids" are baby goats, and as I have children of my own, the similarities are not lost on me. The mama goat will paw the ground like she's making a nest. We might see her rub her abdomen against a tree to move the kid into place, she might even stretch, doing a funny sort of goat yoga, downward dog meets cat pose, to move her young near the birth canal. One particular spring, about ten years ago, I noticed that mama goats do one other remarkable thing.

At that time I was in a raw and honest place in my walk with God. I was wondering if God truly loved human beings. Questions circled the inner landscape of my life. Did God really want us, long for us? Did the character of God's relationship with human beings consist of love and longing? Or was it more like duty and drudgery? My shaky reasoning went something like this: God created us, but we ended up being such a mess that God, out of his own integrity, *had* to deal with us. But in all honesty, God didn't want to, he just wanted to nuke the planet and be done with us.

In the midst of this conversation spring had sprung, and I was out in a tiny lean-to shed with a mama goat who was getting ready to kid. For several days she had been making her nest, pawing the ground, moving dirt and hay around in circles. I often found her rubbing her body against a tree, urging her young into the birth canal. It was just her and me on a chilly spring night, and I could tell that her time had come. All the usual signs were there. I remember that the sky was crystal clear, I could see my breath and hers. The only light was from a headlamp I was wearing, and after several dirty looks from her, I turned it off. Who knew goats can give the stink eye?

About twenty minutes before the baby was born, she began to do one thing that would forever change how I understood God's love and longing. She began to hum or sing or something like it. A soft bleat with her lips closed. It wasn't like a cry as if she was in pain, it was soft and soothing. She continued this "singing" through the contractions, through the pushing, and when, finally, the baby was born, she nuzzled the new life. She licked it clean and continued to sing until the new life sang back.

For the next few hours, as my legs went numb from sitting on a paint can, mama and baby softly, in a very tender way, sang to one another. In this way she marked her baby as hers and the baby knew its mama's voice and sang back. Connection was in the singing. Safety was in the song. God used that moment to speak deep healing and truth into my questions. Our conversation took a monumental shift.

LONGING FOR CONNECTION

Developmental psychologists tell us that every human comes into the world looking, reaching, and longing for connection. They tell us that even within the womb children connect with their mother's voice, their mother's smell, and their mother's heartbeat. After we are born, we search our parents' eyes for connection. When they smile, we smile back. This first smile doesn't mean the same for the babies as it does for the smitten parents: the babies are not pleased or happy; they are mirroring the parents in an effort to connect.[1]

Although this intense desire to connect is an attempt for physical survival, it is also a part of our psychological and spiritual survival. The child who doesn't connect with a primary caregiver by the age of two is likely to develop something called reactive attachment disorder, which is a serious and horribly painful condition in which a person has the longing to connect but is unable.

This longing to connect is woven into every human person. From our first breath we are governed by this longing. My first memorable example of early human longing was when my daughter was born. As soon as she was placed in my husband's outstretched arms, she grabbed onto his finger, which is a Palmer Grasp reflex, I am told. The intense longing to connect is even wired into our reflexes.

But not only are humans wired for longing, we were created from longing. The Creator God longed us into existence. "Before I formed you in the womb I knew you," says Jeremiah 1:5. The psalmist reminds us, "It was you who formed my inward parts; you knit me together in my mother's womb" (Psalm 139:13). And Paul explains that God "chose us in [Christ] before the creation of the world" (Ephesians 1:4 NIV).

Every human has been chosen. God, who needed nothing else to be whole and whose joy was complete before one ounce of creation, longed for you. We human beings often long from a place of brokenness, but God, who is whole and holy, longs from a place of abundance and joy. The parable of the lost sheep found in Matthew 18:10-14 is about longing. It is a story about a shepherd who longs for his sheep so intensely that he leaves the ninety-nine to find the lost one. God has been longing for you, longing to connect with you, since before your very beginning. Every child you know has been longed by God into existence.

We also long for God. Just as we are hardwired to seek connection with our caregivers, we are hardwired to seek connection with God. Lisa Miller, psychology and education professor at Columbia, says, "Biologically, we are hardwired for spiritual connection. Spiritual development is for our species a biological and psychological imperative from birth."[2] This hardwiring pulses in our bodies, in our minds and hearts, compelling us to reach for connection with God.

We get a glimpse of the human wiring to connect in Mark 10:13-16.

People were bringing little children to him in order that he might touch them; and the disciples spoke sternly to them. But when Jesus saw this, he was indignant and said to them, "Let the little children come to me; do not stop them; for it is to such as these that the kingdom of God belongs. Truly I tell you, whoever does not receive the kingdom of God as a little child will never enter it." And he took them up in his arms, laid his hands on them, and blessed them.

Notice Jesus' first word in this passage, "Let." *Let* implies an already forward moving progression. The children are already coming; it is their natural inclination to seek connection. God has been longing, is longing now, and will continue to long for children, and, further, children are wired to long right back. The movement is already at hand.

What begins with forward motion continues on to what will hinder. Jesus says, "do not stop them," which could be an indictment of the ministries for children and youth in the past and in our time. The past teachings of the church for training children in the way of Christ were created and implemented with good intention. However, many of these intentions have fallen short of acknowledging the full humanity of children or God's capacity to meet children precisely where they are.

When we adults fall into broken patterns of thinking about children and about God, we tend to move toward models of babysitting, entertainment, or, worse, manipulation through shame and fear. Jesus seems to be asking less of the adult and more of the child. Jesus seems to be inviting the adult to empower the child and move out of the way. He is inviting the child to direct encounter.

A BROKEN PATTERN OF CONNECTION

My first conscious memory of God was in the La Sal Mountains in Utah. I was with my family and we had driven up and into the timber from our tiny town of Moab to cut firewood for the coming winter. As the adults began their work, I wandered off into a grove of aspen trees. If you've never seen aspens in autumn, imagine gold coins, suspended by tiny gossamer strings, glistening in the sunshine.

Aspen trees grow in groves. Underneath, in the dark richness of the soil, they are connected to one another by their life-giving root system. They live in close proximity to each other, and while each is a single tree, they are also a community. They share their health and their sickness. And on this particular day they seemed to be issuing me an invitation. I was only five years old but can still remember the sponginess of the ground, which was damp with morning dew and squishy from years of healthy cycles of decomposition. I bounded my way into the aspens' presence.

All at once I had a sense of awe and perhaps glory. The space was so lovely, so inviting. I remember being drawn in. I wanted more of whatever this was, so I lay down on my back in their midst. I gazed up at the little coins, squinting from the intense brightness of the sun. It seemed like the earth itself was breathing, and I was breathing with it: slow and deep breathing of indescribable sweetness. A long-known reality began to be realized in me that day. I gradually understood that I was not alone. I can't explain how I knew this, and I certainly couldn't articulate that knowledge then, but I distinctly remember knowing that I was not alone, I had never been alone, and that whatever, whoever, was with me, loved me.

Fast-forward six years and my life was much different. A big family move to Texas and the daily comings and goings buried this experience in my memory. At the Christian school I attended, I sat at a tiny, isolated desk, surrounded by thin booklets of math, science, spelling, reading, all the usual culprits. I felt myself being swallowed by loneliness. The intellectual pursuits doled out to me in four-page increments were no salve for my soul. Each student was required to have a Bible in their possession and to memorize an assigned passage of Scripture each month. They were mostly passages around what Dallas Willard calls "sin management."

In the midst of drudgery, curiosity and, I suspect, the gentle guidance of the Spirit led me to the Gospels, and I found a name for that someone who was with me in the aspens. I don't remember what story of Jesus captured my heart first. All I can remember is an insatiable desire to be with this person Jesus. I grew to love him. My imagination was enlivened by his life, my heart was broken by his death, and hope found a source in his resurrection. I refused to complete my other assignments; all I wanted to do was read about, talk about, and, yes, even write minisermons about Jesus.

The universe of my little desk with my Bible was safe and full of life. The generous gospel was the lifeblood of this universe. It was in stark contrast to the rest of my world. The implicit theology of the school and the church was that all human beings are isolated from God unless they have spoken the words of confession until they had been broken by their sin and begged God to forgive them. To be sure, this was a lived reality for many adults, but God was as near as the breath in my lungs, and I had already grown to love him.

As an adult I understand why it was done, and I can empathize with the driving need to control outcomes. If theology is rooted in scarcity and logical conclusions lead to a fear that children will burn in Dante's eternal fires of hell, there is no time to muck about with loving relationship. The children have got to be "saved" through any means. And that's what happened. Manipulative and coercive means were used to convince the children to walk the aisle and say the prayer. This, we were assured, would save us from the impending devastation. My young mind understood that if I didn't comply, I would be alone again. My family would be ripped away by the Jesus I had grown to love. Seeds of distrust were sown in my heart.

This must surely be what Jesus meant when he said, "Let the children come to me and *do not stop* them." When fear is used to manipulate outcomes, it will cause a full stop. Danger doesn't draw; it drives. Jesus was well aware of the adult propensity to control. Even in this passage his disciples are "speaking sternly" in an attempt to control the situation. Jesus does not put up with it. He is indignant and commands the adults to back down.

LONGING FOR GOD

What did Jesus know about children? That they are already drawn to connect with God. That coercion is a short-term, highly damaging solution to behavior management. That every person, especially a child, is wired to long for God. That direct encounter with the Father would change everything. He knew how to tap into this longing. He knew how to listen people to life.

I have seen this many times as I sit with children as a listening friend at Haven House. Our ministry is called holy listening, which is a period of time set apart for an adult to sit with a child and listen. Together the adult and the child listen to the life of the child, discerning where God has been showing up. On one particular day I was meeting with Sadie, who was ten. She and her mother had moved into Haven House seven months earlier. It was the longest she had ever lived in the same place. For many years they lived in their car, driving from Walmart parking lot to Walmart parking lot. At Haven House, Sadie was in school and had regular meals and a community surrounding her, but she still was struggling. She was contentious with the other residents, explosive with the staff, and rarely at rest in her body. The dedicated care providers at Haven House got Sadie into counseling, which helped.

Sadie also wanted to come to holy listening. Most weeks I sat with Sadie and listened to the disjointed stories of her life. In holy listening we sit on a white blanket as a sign of sacred space. Sadie entered the room with me but sat just outside of the blanket. This was her choice, and I honored it with no protest. After several weeks of meeting, I wondered how Sadie might respond to the Imago Dei Ministries Reflection Cards.[3] The Reflection Cards are the brainchild of therapist Katie Skurja. The deck of cards contains photographs of superheroes, fictional cartoon characters, and other objects on which to project thoughts and feelings. We opened our time in the usual way: she sat just outside of the blanket, and I asked for grace. I introduced the Reflection Cards and invited Sadie to choose two cards that told a story about a time she knew God was with her.

Sadie chose her cards and arranged them in a shallow sandbox we used to draw prayers. "Can you tell me these stories," I asked, pointing to the cards. She introduced her stories with the caveat that "these are not from today but over a while." She told the story of a bullying incident that made her afraid. "But it wasn't the scariest." She went on to say, "The scariest was the day my dad and brother got in a fight." I asked, "Where was God during the fight?" "Oh, he was there," she said. "Only no one could hear him." With the next card she told the story of swinging at school and singing. She described how God was all around her, lifting her up, and singing with her. "He likes it when I sing," she said. Then she shifted her focus to drawing patterns with her fingers in the sand around her pictures. She asked if she could use the blocks in the sand too. I agreed that it was a brilliant idea. "You can use this time to talk with God about your stories," I offered. She nodded her head and then asked if she could move our battery-powered candle to the sand too.

Slowly, she moved her entire body onto the blanket and created her own prayer collage out of her stories, the sand, and our candle. This Jesus, who knows that children are wired to connect, reached out his hand and drew her to himself.

SOAKING IT IN

The following are suggested topics for conversation with God, with others, or even with yourself.

- Reflect on your first experience of God. How did this experience shape what you believe about God today?

- Meditate on the version of Psalm 23 found in appendix 1. Notice what stirs in you. What resonates with your soul? What seems to be too good to be true?

- Reflect on your own childhood spirituality. Was it shaped by a theology of scarcity or generosity? What do you think about that today?

- Reflect on your relationship with Jesus over the course of your life. How has it grown or changed as time has passed?

two

CHILDREN'S SPIRITUAL FORMATION

Childhood is openness. Human childhood is infinite openness.

KARL RAHNER

WE CAN GET A GLIMPSE of how children perceive God simply by asking them to draw a picture of God. Typically, God is drawn as male and usually is floating in the sky. Children who have been to church in North America might draw God as a white Jesus-like figure on the cross. It is rare for a child to draw God as the trinitarian Community of Love. Many of our churches and all of our pop culture, which has a formational influence, haven't gotten the memo that God is triune. If connection to a community is at the heart of our longing for God, but our picture of God is of a lone ranger floating in the sky, our desire falls short. It misses its mark, and we are left pining for the Community of Love in vain. Children's spiritual formation is the process of living into relationship with the triune God.

THE TRINITARIAN COMMUNITY OF LOVE

God the Father, God the Son, and God the Spirit is Love's Family, and children are on a journey of awaking to their membership within this family. Learning of and leaning into Love's Family is at the heart of spiritual formation with children. Acknowledging and encountering the reality of God as the trinitarian presence is an important step toward developing a theology of children's Christian spiritual formation.

Consider figure 2.1, which was drawn by Annie, an eight-year-old girl. Annie has grown up in a church that practices the prayers of the people in the name of the "Father, and of the Son, and of the Holy Spirit." She heard these words first as a baby and now has

Figure 2.1. "God is like a musical chord. All three and all one."

learned to say them herself. These words accompany a bodily movement of making the sign of the cross. With each sound heard, each word spoken, and each bodily movement, she is engaging the reality of Love's Family. To Annie, music speaks deeply of God, so when she was asked to draw a picture of God, she drew the three primary members of Love's Family playing piano together. When asked about her drawing, Annie said, "God is like a musical chord. All three and all one." Annie is in good company as sixteenth-century Christian mystic Ignatius of Loyola also thought of the Trinity as a musical triad. About her image Annie explained that music is not "by yourself," everyone can play or sing or dance. Within Annie's image of God there is community, there is connection, and there is invitation.

Out of the overflow of joy-filled music and in an act of invitation, which comes from the center of their communal existence, the trinitarian God creates. Whatever the trinitarian God creates is infused with God's image. Since God's image is good, what God creates embodies the potential for every good in the universe (Genesis 1:26-27). Let that sink in for a moment. Every human is created with the potential for every good in the universe. God does not create from a deficit but from wholeness. God is a Community of Love, and because children are created by that community, they bear the mark of their Creator. And that mark is the *imago Dei*.

The union of image and likeness, found in Genesis 1:26, has been known as the imago Dei. It is something like a homing beacon. In part the imago Dei is the breath of God breathed into every human person who has ever lived. It is deep calling to deep. Whenever a child encounters beauty, truth, or goodness in the world, this beacon sounds. It echoes in the souls of children as a reminder that they were created from loving community and belong in loving community.

Once when I was trying (and floundering) to communicate this idea to a group of adolescent boys, they met me more than halfway by offering a modern metaphor. "Lacy, it's like when you lose your phone," one explained. "You know how you can ping your phone with the computer and it will ping back? Is that what it's like?" They were spot on. It *is* like that. Every child has been wired with longing and enlivened with the breath of God, so when a child encounters goodness, truth, or beauty, the child's soul pings. There is a resonance that draws them toward the Community of Love.

Irenaeus, a second-century church father, has been paraphrased as saying, "The Glory of God is a human being fully alive." God's glory is revealed in a child becoming increasingly aware, increasingly alive. John reminds us, "All things came into being through him, and without him not one thing came into being. What has come into being in him was life, and the life was the light of all people" (John 1:3-4). Patrick Henry Reardon explains that Irenaeus's quote is not a treatise for self-fulfillment as it is often interpreted.[1] Instead, Irenaeus is arguing that a growing awareness of Christ in the world coincides with greater human living. Every human being experiences some measure of this awareness. The imago Dei breathed into children continually calls them into a participatory awareness of the God who surrounds them. As Dallas Willard states, "We are, all of us, never-ceasing spiritual beings with a unique calling to count for good in God's great universe."[2]

This should not surprise us because the Trinity functions and conceives in love. A child's experience of God is an expression of that love. As children are wired both to receive love and are themselves rich in love, they are especially able to experience God. Jesus made it clear that children are welcomed to experience God. Humanity's beginning is not at the fall but at creation, where we are loved of God. Becoming awake to God, to their own belovedness, and the belovedness of others is a child's lifelong journey into the heart of the Community of Love. An adult can participate in a child's awakening by being a listening presence, but the adult cannot make the journey for the child. They can help a child recognize and respond to Love's divine invitation, but they cannot force sight or connection.

Children's spiritual formation is the journey of becoming aware of God and participating in the trinitarian reality. As Annie showed in her drawing and explanation, spiritual formation is learning to hear the music and accepting the invitation to participate. The modern term *spiritual formation* takes into account recent physiological and psychological understandings of three formative influences on human spiritual development. First, an outside influence, which can include training and teaching (often referred to as nurture). Second, the genetic predisposition to relationship children are born with (nature). Third, the outcome of the choices humans make throughout life (human will or agency). Every child is shaped by these influences. Thus, every child receives spiritual formation.

Shaped by Encounter

For over fifteen hundred years the Christian tradition has discussed, articulated, and prescribed training models, strategies, and doctrines that have emphasized knowledge about God. The goal of teaching children was to guide them into mental assent and moral knowledge. While knowledge about someone is good to have, it does not lead to friendship. For example, I know about Archbishop Desmond Tutu. I have read many of his books and listened to his lectures. His teachings have inspired me and directed my moral compass. But we don't have a relationship; we don't hang out. While I admire him greatly, proximity has placed limitations on friendship. However, God is not limited by proximity.

God is near and longs to connect with children. Experiential knowledge helps children develop a relationship with God. The children's spirituality movement of the last hundred years has opened the discussion to include the direct knowledge of the Trinity's presence, which children gain through experience. In essence we learn to play music with the Trinity not only by reading the music or biographies about the musicians but by grabbing our finger cymbals and giving it a go!

Children's spiritual formation has four elements that shape and form a child's relationship with the trinitarian Community of Love.

ELEMENTS OF SPIRITUAL FORMATION

God's self. From a human's birth and on, God is constantly inviting human beings into relationship. God has given God's self to this relationship endeavor with humans. Through the homing beacon, through wired longing for connection, and through the pings lovingly woven within our world, God gives God's self to every person. While goodness, beauty, and truth are God's fingerprints in the world, God also has others. Whenever children experience wonder, as in *I wonder why bees like pink flowers?* we hear the ping of invitation. Children are born scientists hungry with curiosity. Whenever children feel a sense of awe or hallowed mystery, their souls ping.

Edward Robinson's book *The Original Vision* describes some of the ways people have encountered God's presence as children. In a study of over four thousand stories in which adults reflected on their religious experience or spiritual awareness, 15 percent of the stories told occurred in childhood and affected the life of the person. These participants interpreted their experiences of goodness, beauty, truth, wonder, mystery, and awe as encounters with the divine. Far from being spectacular, these experiences were woven into the ordinariness of life.[3]

It seems that these experiences occurred in three learning spaces. The space of *tears*, where there is brokenness, suffering, and pain. The space of *nature*, which is the first "book" we are given to experience the revelation of God. And in the *thin space* or threshold, where events and information sync in an unexpected way, where woven cords of meaning surprisingly connect. These are some of the pings that remind children that they were created by the Community of Love for the Community of Love.

Many children who live at Haven House are bursting with gratitude when they sit with me. The stability of place is a welcomed gift of grace, and though they struggle to know how to negotiate the sameness of daily life, they are grateful for the consistent nourishment of food and shelter. For Amanda, though, living at the shelter didn't feel like grace and light. She had lived with her grandmother most of her life, but when her mother got out of jail and her grandmother died, she was forced to reconcile a relationship long severed. With all the loss that surrounded her previous six months, isolation and loneliness threatened to overwhelm her. I asked her where she saw God showing up in her day, beginning with her walk to the bus stop in the early morning.

Cottonwood trees as it turns out pointed her to God. It was autumn and their yellow leaves falling to the ground helped her count her losses. "I think God cries with me," she said one day when reflecting on her grandmother's death. As winter came and snow covered the ground and the bare cottonwood branches still reached to the sky, she drew pictures of the trees and wrote the words *peace, tears, bright,* and *quiet.* Something was shifting in Amanda, but I was not privy to the details. Her audience was with God; I was only invited to witness what she offered. Spring came and Amanda began to not only talk about the buds on the trees but she embodied hope in the future that she didn't previously have. She held her body more lightly, she smiled more, and she laughed easier. Nature, more specifically cottonwood trees, echoed the ping that drew her to God and out of her loneliness.

Relationships in human living. These pings occur in a child's everyday life. A life filled with curiosity and play, of new experiences and boundaries, of connections and separations is what God seeks to share with a child. Life, the second element of spiritual formation, offers opportunities to encounter God through relationships with other people through nature, art, wonder, and mystery. Relationships with adults are an essential part of a child's life that shape and form what a child believes about God. A child's picture of God is formed in the beginning by the most powerful adults in their lives.

These powerful adults can be parents, teachers, pastors, or other family members. Relational connections establish patterns of trust and lay a foundation for expectations of love and acceptance. Often the most tangible example of unconditional love to a child is their relationship with a loving grandparent. The attention and care that grandparents offer to children have the potential to shape a loving and attentive image of God in the mind and heart of a child. Grandparents can embody a slower posture that frees them for endless listening with delight to children. Further, they embody timeworn wisdom and humility through which children sense an authentic love and generosity.

I acknowledge that many folks have not had loving adult experiences. Not all adults embody the love and delight of God. If this is true for you, it might be helpful to reflect on your picture of God in light of your painful adult experience. Talking with a counselor, spiritual director, or close friend can help to bring healing.

Pain in human living. Children also encounter God through the woundedness of human existence. Even in pain, perhaps especially in pain, children can become open to the healing presence of Love's Family. The first days of school can stir up fear in children. They can seem like "terrifying dragons." This was the description given to me by Jeremy. The first day of third grade was bad enough, but the first day of school in a new school in a new town was "terrifying." When I asked Jeremy to describe what terrifying felt like, he said, "like a dragon looking at you just waiting to eat you." After a bit more sharing about his sense of "terrifying," I asked Jeremy if he wanted to use the finger labyrinth to talk with God about this dragon. He did. As per our usual prayer ritual, Jeremy moved his finger through the labyrinth and talked to God about the dragon. When Jeremy's finger reached the center, he breathed three deep breaths for God the Father, God the Son, and God the Spirit. Then he moved his finger through the labyrinth to the outside, listening for God's personal communication to him.

When Jeremy arrived at the outside, he looked up at me and smiled. I asked, "Would you like to share what you heard from God? Sometimes what God says to us is private but sometimes it's not, and if you want to share it, I'm glad to listen." Jeremy nodded his head. "God said I don't have to be afraid of dragons because he is the dragon fighter." "Am I hearing you say that you aren't afraid anymore?" I responded. Jeremy corrected me, "No! Dragons have big teeth, but God is going to school with me, and God's not afraid." I asked, "What do you think you might do to remember that God is with you at school?" At first Jeremy shrugged his shoulders, then after a bit of brainstorming together we came up with the idea of holding three fingers on his belly when the butterflies remind him he's afraid: one finger for God the Father, one for God the Son, and one for God the Spirit. This small act of prayer formed Jeremy. It reminded him that he was created for more than fear, and that Love's Family would face down every dragon with him.

While belovedness in light of God's fullness is where children begin, their wounds are not far off. Children will discover that, unlike the trinitarian God whose image they contain, they lack both the knowledge and ability to actualize every potential good (Romans 6:1-14). Human woundedness, both our own and the wounds of those around us, is a roadblock to our participation in God's reality of truth, beauty, and goodness. Though children are beloved by God and invited into communion with God, the wounds of human living cause them to recoil in fear. Fear is the essence of these roadblocks. Fear is at the heart of the very first roadblock story told in the Bible (Genesis 3). Fear whispers distrust and eats away at relationships of trust.

The journey of becoming awake and participatory in the trinitarian reality is a journey through fear. Adults often forget that children's woundedness and the fear it inspires to their detriment are roadblocks to communion that are set up as early as the first wounds are experienced. Further we are often undone by the existential fears of children. A child's fears remind us of our own fears that we have worked hard to bury or rationalize. They also remind us of our limited reach. Adults can't always make things better; we can't fix the larger world or the inner world of a child.

Children haven't learned to bury their fears, and as of yet they can't rationalize them. In the vulnerability that these fears invite, children are drawn to connecting with the One who can speak love to their fear. Over the course of their lives children have the chance for hundreds of these connections. They may experience one major connection and several reconnections afterward.

The life of Jesus. Knowing that connection is at the heart of relationship, God took on flesh and "moved into the neighborhood" (John 1:14 *The Message*). The life, death, and resurrection of Jesus are not only redemptive but also formational. For centuries we have focused on the importance of children connecting with the death and resurrection of Jesus but missed the basic element of connection found in Jesus' life. Jesus' incarnation offers a "withness" children can connect through. Although Christ has always been and will always be, his incarnation had a human relational purpose to it; his life with a body demonstrated a shared experience of humanity and intimate human relationship. His bodily mortal life serves as both an invitation into and an example of intimate community.

By his model Jesus shows children how to enter and live in the Community of Love. Children are invited to experience Jesus in his own life through the Gospels because Jesus is infinitely relatable to children. Once when taking a group of middle school children through Luke 2:41-52, a teen boy commented, "I get that. My mom says, 'Child, why have you treated us like this?' all the time. My parents don't get me either."

Jesus faced the same existential fears all humans face, but these fears never took root in his soul. He knew how to connect with Love's Family so completely that love overcame his fear. As a member of the trinitarian reality, Jesus exudes love and is love. Like all human beings, he experienced growth into love, spurred on by intentionally walking as closely with the Father as possible.

Spiritual practices. Jesus also modeled that other form of knowledge—training—by practicing prayer, solitude, celebration, and the like. Prayer, solitude, and celebration are among the intentional practices directed toward a deeper connection with God and others. These practices can take the form of classical spiritual practices like those described by Richard Foster in *Celebration of Discipline* and Valerie Hess and Marti Watson Garlett's *Habits of a Child's Heart*. Spiritual practices are a means of grace, a conduit of transforming love and friendship that draws children further into the heart of love for God and neighbor. Jesus practiced them and so can children.

Children pray; they enter into conversation with God. Children meditate, focus their minds on God, and listen for their own inner voice. Children can choose to let go of things that keep them from increased awareness of Love's Family. Children have an extraordinary capacity to serve others; they can give up getting their own way. Children desire solitude and guidance. They long to be known by telling the truth about themselves. Each of these basic spiritual practices opens an ordinary sacred space for a child to reach their hand toward God and find that God is already there.

Children's spiritual formation unites all four formational elements: God's self, human living, Jesus' life, and spiritual practices. Children engage all the dimensions of the self when they participate. They are natural celebrators, and they revel in responding to love's extravagant invitation. In essence, children are wired for worship. I learned this in a tiny Church of the Nazarene.

The shift from hymns to praise choruses was a rough one in this rural, mostly older congregation. To be sure, the hymns marked the faith stories of many of the congregants, and so giving them up bordered on heresy. This particular Sunday the preschoolers processed into the church and straight up the aisle to the front pew. The children's pastor decided that they needed to be present and participating in worship rather than stuck in the nursery. And participate they did.

It's interesting how the bodies of the dour can betray their owners when children are involved. The worship pastor began leading with the praise song *Marvelous Light*. By the end of the first verse the children had broken loose from their neat and tidy little row. They were singing with all they were worth and dancing to boot. Their joy and worship could not be hidden in their bodies. By the second verse something began to happen to the adults standing behind them. First, there was a bit of swaying and then some clapping. Dour turned to delight as the children led the church into worship. Love's Community played the song; the children heard the invitation and they danced.

Soaking It In

The following are suggested topics for conversation with God, with others, or even with yourself.

- In your imagination hold a picture of yourself as a young child. With your nondominant hand draw a picture of an early experience of goodness, beauty, truth, wonder, awe, or mystery.

- Reflect on your picture of God. If you were to draw a picture of God, what would it look like? Feel free to create a collage of your picture of God. Begin by choosing colors that represent your feelings about God. Then lean into creative freedom. Use images from magazines, shapes, and symbols.

- Notice what aspects of your picture of God are not reflected in the life and character of Jesus.

- Notice what aspects of your picture of God have changed over time.

- Older adults within a congregation are often overlooked when it comes to children's ministry. What would it look like within your congregation if a group of older adults decided to make it their mission to listen the little children to life?

three

POSTURE, POWER,
AND PATTERNS

Every child you encounter is a divine appointment.

WES STAFFORD, COMPASSION INTERNATIONAL

To BE THE GREATEST IS TO command the power in the room. In 1964 boxing legend Cassius Clay, now known as Muhammad Ali, declared that he was the greatest, in a clear move to command power as he prepared to challenge Sonny Liston for the world title. Two decades later greatness and power were again up for grabs on a smaller scale, but the struggle was similar. While playing at her grandparents' home, four-year-old Jenny dumped a jar of pennies on the floor. Her parents and grandparents watched with delight as she played with them, making tall and short stacks, comparing the tiny numbers only her young eyes could clearly see.

Then it became time to pick up the pennies and go home. Jenny didn't want to pick up the pennies or go home. Jenny's parents wanted the pennies picked up; it was time to go home. They wanted obedience. The power struggle was on.

The struggle for power is an old one. The Synoptic Gospels all record a scrap between the disciples over who was the greatest. In one account James and John even got their mother in on the power grab. Jesus taught that there could be a different pattern for power. The disciples struggled to wrap their minds and their bodies around this new reality. Jesus, knowing that bodies are "personal power packages" created to carry out the will of the human spirit, offered his struggling friends a bodily example of another way to deal with power.[1] He brought a child into their midst.

> An argument arose among them as to which one of them was the greatest. But Jesus, aware of their inner thoughts, took a little child and put it by his side, and said to them, "Whoever welcomes this child in my name welcomes me, and whoever welcomes me welcomes the one who sent me; for the least among all of you is the greatest." (Luke 9:46-48)

The struggle for power goes all the way back to Eve and Adam in Eden. Why would God, who clearly has all the power, yield his power for a chance at relationship with the very beings he created? Eve and Adam had an intimate relationship with God and with each other until the seeds of mistrust prompted them to use their human will to exchange relationship for the power to rule. The destructive power pattern is about who will rule, who is in control, who is the greatest. The power structure Jesus was helping his disciples learn is about relationship.

The God who generously gave human beings their power to choose (will) is in pursuit of human relationship, not human rule.

In an act of grace God placed in all of humanity an essential orientation toward relationship. The most powerful drive a child has is for relationship.

While Jenny clearly did not want to pick up the pennies—using her will to pursue her rule—her deeper longing was one of relationship. Jenny's father knew this. He knew that her deepest desire was to connect with those who love her. So instead of ordering her to pick up the pennies while he watched, he sat down on the floor next to her and asked if he could pick them up with her. While scooping them together Jenny's dad asked, "What did you like about playing with the pennies?" This created an opening for Jenny and her father to connect. Jenny's father learned more about her, and Jenny was reminded again that she was loved.

Notice how Jesus and Jenny's dad shifted the power with their bodies. Jesus put the child by his side, offering his body as an ally for sharing power, a new power pattern. Jenny's dad sat on the floor with his daughter; he moved into her space. Notice that Jesus shared the power of his social structure, "whoever welcomes this child . . . welcomes me." Then in a concluding blow to the pursuit of power to rule, Jesus offered this memorable line "the least among all of you is the greatest."

With these power packages, bodies, we participate in a pattern of power. There is a movement and exchange of power in every human interaction. As we seek to engage in spiritual conversations with children, we must be cognizant of the power in the room, and like Jesus, if we want relationship rather than rule, we must shift the power.

POSTURE AND POWER

While engaging spiritual conversations with children, the listening adult assumes the relational posture of an attentive listener, which is communicated through her body. Keep in mind that the difference in bodily size combined with the sociocultural expressions of authority solidify the fact that child and adult do not meet on equal authoritative ground. To engender the kind of open conversational relationship necessary for spiritual conversations, the adult needs to create a physical and spiritual space that fosters equal authoritative power as much as possible. We've got to shift the power.

Authoritative power is not expressed through bodily size alone; it is also found in the choice to engage in spiritual conversations in the first place. While we can invite and encourage children, the ultimate power of choosing lies with the child. In a formal listening session the child is given power by having the freedom to determine how long the session is, within a twenty to forty-five-minute framework. Thus, the freedom to choose, the freedom to use their will, becomes a tool to equalize the power between the adult and the child. The power to choose when and how to have conversations adds meaning to the spiritual life of a child.

Another way of shifting power is to sit on the floor with the child. Western forms of education have trained children to sit in chairs, which restricts movement and bodily expression. Children often prefer being on the floor, partly because they can control how close they want to be to the adult. In my own ministry I utilize a white blanket dotted with green leaves to create a sacred space. The child and I take off our shoes and step onto the blanket at the same time, entering the sacred space together. Were I to be on the blanket first, my prior presence would communicate greater authority, potentially setting up a roadblock to intimate communication and experience with God.

When children lead the play and the dialogue, the power also shifts. I had been meeting with William each week for two months. Throughout our time he easily learned the rhythms of spiritual conversation. He shared his thoughts and feelings, engaged prayer practices, and then during our fifth session he finally told his truth. "I really don't like this," he said as he let out a heavy sigh. "What is it that you don't like?" I inquired. "All the talking. I wish we did something else," he said, relieved. I happened to be carrying around Jenga blocks in my holy listening bag. Jenga is a mindless game in which players stack and restack rectangle blocks until the tower falls over and one person is declared a winner. We were using the blocks to build the inn in the Nativity story.

In what surely was Spirit inspired, I thanked him for his honesty and asked him if he wanted to play the game instead. A resounding yes broke through the reluctance of the moment. During our two rounds of Jenga, stories and details about his week and where he had noticed God flowed from him. He spoke of moments of anxiety and anger with a depth I had not yet known. William taught me about power and about the magic of the third thing. For many people direct conversation is loaded with pressure. The pressure looks like swirling thoughts of what to say, when to say it, and at a deeper level even what to actually think or feel and why is that so. Children also experience this inner tumult. With all the inner ruckus it is not safe for the soul of the child to engage, and so it doesn't.

Enter Jenga or the third thing. A third thing is something mostly unrelated to the conversation at hand. It offers a place to funnel anxiety so that the authentic conversation can occur. As we played this game, William's active thoughts had somewhere to go, something to do. My intuition is that he wanted to share a bit of his inner world with me but couldn't wade through his thoughts and feelings. Once those active thoughts were settled doing something else, he could speak about his soul. He could tell his stories of anger, anxiety, and God. I also learned about the power differential inherent in spiritual conversations with children. It took him two months, which is five sessions, to muster up the courage to speak his truth. Time is the ultimate test of safety. While I hope that all the embedded measures of leveling the power differential offer freedom, it takes time to test the message being communicated. William took a brave step toward his own will, and it paid off.

In his research Brendan Hyde, professor and children's spirituality researcher, found that "a conversation works most effectively when the subject matter of the conversation assumes control, while those in dialogue allow themselves to be led by it."[2] Children are accustomed to adults leading, so allowing children to lead in both play and dialogue requires engaging questions, patience, and silence. Children are thirsty to be heard, but it may take a moment or two of silence in order for them to feel like they can fill the space with their thoughts and feelings, ultimately with their own power to be heard. Depending on the age and personality of the child, it may take months of sessions for this to become natural and easy.

A PREDICTABLE PATTERN

There is a predictable pattern to spiritual conversations with children. The pattern utilizes two natural movements that can be found in growing human-to-human relationships, the movement to recognize and the movement to respond. It is important to note that in children these movements will be uniquely childlike. Goodness, truth, beauty, wonder, and mystery are all means by which God is building a relationship with children; therefore they will be interwoven within both movements. Ivy Beckwith and David Csinos remind us in their book *Children's Ministry in the Way of Jesus* that the "transcendent God showers all people with grace by giving us the immeasurable gift of the capacity to know God, to sense the very presence of God and to enter into a real, life-forming relationship with God."[3] In spiritual conversations with children, the listening adult makes room for the child to recognize God's presence and respond to this recognition.

While this is the natural pattern, barriers to this pattern do begin to develop. Human beings are habitual, therefore when children begin to recognize God's activity, they will respond in the way they have responded to significant people in their lives. For children the people who have most affected their lives are often one or both of their parents, grandparents, and siblings. A child's picture of God is in part formed from their interactions with their most dominant parent.

Children will most respond to God in the pattern they have responded to this parent. The response may be closed or open or most likely somewhere in between. A child's picture of God entangled with their picture of their parents or grandparents can be life-giving when the relationship is safe, nurturing, and loving. Other times when the picture doesn't reflect the character of Christ, harm to a child's view of God can and does occur. This picture shapes both the ability to recognize God's presence and the way in which children respond.

While this developmental pattern is generally true, I have also heard children and adults whose closest relationships are painful tell of an experience with God that transcended the struggle. In a mystery far beyond me, the Spirit differentiates God's self from the unhealthy relationship in a subtle degree for all children and in a dramatic way for others. For some children it may be unarticulated knowing that there is more to God than what they see in their parents. For others it may be as vivid as the following story told by an adult as she reflected back on her childhood self.

With a father who was a sergeant in the military and a mother who was miserable in her marriage, how could I have a picture of God that was loving or even joyful? But I did, mainly because of a dream I had. One morning when I was about four years old, I woke after a dream with this loving parent-type person. In my dream we were playing on the swing together. I loved that dream so much that I tried to hold it in my mind before going to bed each night. On some nights I did have more encounters with this person in my dreams. In one dream I remember, this person took care of me when I was sick, and I also remember eating meals together. Eventually, I quit having those dreams, but even now as I think about it, I can see that my picture of God was shaped by "this person" that I was interacting with in my dreams.

Spiritual conversations with children embody the opportunity to lay down patterns of open embrace toward God and create new patterns of response if needed. Children can learn to hear the voice of God and respond before the baggage of adulthood begins to mar their hearing and close them off. When children are invited to listen and look for the movement of God in their life, it is a tangible reminder that they are not alone and opens them to the possibility of resiliency when life feels overwhelming. Empathy is the connective tissue of living relationships. Helping a child recognize that God is not only with them but feels alongside them is an antidote to shame and isolation.

While recognition is the first movement, responding is the second movement in spiritual conversations with children. The will of the child comes alive through response. Through the engagement of agency, a child's desire for God sets a living fire for relationship. The adult listener can invite children to respond by making available ways to respond that both honor childhood and include all the dimension of a child. Children, like all people, must choose, and they must choose without manipulation. The wooing of the heart is the Spirit's modus operandi. The frailty and freedom of choosing are honored by the Spirit, and we can do no less.

It is important to remember that these movements are not linear or sequential. Recognizing and responding can happen all at once or each at a time. For children, even telling their story and their feelings about the story is response. We accompany children on their journey with fear and trembling because we are aware that their picture of God is in part formed by us. The listening adult is to stay fully present to each movement of recognition and keep the space open and hospitable for response. As Sofia Cavalletti puts it so well, "We are responding to the child's silent request: 'Help me to come closer to God by myself.'"[4]

NOTICING THE RHYTHM: SPIRITUAL DIRECTION WITH KAREN

The pattern of recognizing and responding can be seen more clearly in a listening session. In the following section you are invited to experience snippets of three spiritual conversations with Karen. All of Karen's identifying details, as well as the subject matter, have been changed to protect our agreement of confidentiality. As you engage notice the pattern of recognition and response.

Session 1. Karen is eight years old. At our first meeting Karen entered the room, took off her shoes, and immediately began to ask questions about what she saw. I told her that we were meeting so that I could listen to her. Together we would listen for what she and God had been doing together. She eagerly nodded her head. Because I knew that Karen regularly attended church, I felt free to use the God language she was comfortable with. The following conversation began after several minutes of choosing an image and playing with the battery-powered candle.

LACY. (*Pointing to a picture of Jesus and a boy from the* Jesus Storybook Bible *that is on the tiny easel.*) Do you know who that is?

KAREN. That is Jesus and a boy. I like that picture. I like how Jesus is winking.

LACY. What is it about the wink that you like?

KAREN. It's like that Jesus is fun. No, funny, like he's telling a joke. I like funny people. You're funny too. (*Smiles at me, looking me in the eyes.*)

(*I wonder if she is seeking to connect with me and is hoping to please me. I know that pleasing adults is on the minds of most children. I smile back at her, hoping to reassure her that indeed I like her and want to connect with her.*)

LACY. What do you think of the candle below it?

KAREN. It's not a real candle.

LACY. (*Chuckling at her statement. Children know a fake. They can spot a fake candle, a fake threat, a fake person, and a fake sentiment. It is a reminder that I will need to be as real—as authentic—as I can.*) Yep, you are right, but the church doesn't want us to use a real candle. So, what do you think about using this one? (*Picks up the candle and turns it on.*) It reminds us that God is with us too.

KAREN. I like it. (*Places it next to the picture of Jesus.*) What's all that stuff?

LACY. (*Pulls the box of holy listening stones over to us. Hospital chaplain to children Leanne Hadley created "listening stones" as a way to open up sacred conversation with children.[5] Listening stones are small, smooth river rocks with random symbols printed on them.*) Well, these stones can help you talk and help me listen. You choose three stones that tell about your day or tell about when you are worried or tell about where you are meeting God. Wanna try?

KAREN. (*Already digging in the box, going over each stone carefully and making little comments about each stone.*) Okay. These three. (*Chooses*

45

the following stones and places them in the following order: (1) eyes closed stone, (2) smile stone, (3) foot stone.)

LACY. Would you like to tell me the story of these stones?

KAREN. Well, this one (*picks up the first stone*) is happy eyes. I am happy to be here with you. And the next one is a smile this way but a frown this way (*flips the rock around*). It's a frown because I don't like the dusty tests at school.

LACY. The dusty tests?

KAREN. You know the ones at school. We always have to do them, and I cry, and I hate them.

LACY. You cry and hate them? What makes them dusty?

KAREN. They are boring and hard and stupid. And I worry about them.

LACY. You worry about them?

KAREN. (*Pauses for a few seconds.*) I flip around in my bed.

LACY. At night, when you go to sleep?

KAREN. Yeah. And my mom says, "Go to sleep." But I flip around and bite my nails. (*Shows me her fingers.*) But then I remember that God is with me at school too. So, then I go to sleep.

LACY. What reminds you that God is with you?

KAREN. My nightlight, like this light. (*Picks up and tosses around our battery-powered candle.*)

LACY. What does it feel like when you remember that God is with you?

KAREN. It's like, *Ahh! I'm okay.*

LACY. Do you ever remember at school too?

KAREN. Sometimes. When I'm like *Ahh!*

LACY. What do you do?

KAREN. I say, "Help me with this test."

LACY. Does it work?

KAREN. Yep. (*Flips the smiley stone back to a smiley face.*) See this one, this is when I'm happy.

LACY. Tell me about that?

(*Notice that Karen abruptly shifts the topic. It is normal for children to bounce around from topic to topic. It is important for listening adults to have their sea legs and be able to stay right at the elbow of the child wherever the child may bounce. While I wonder why Karen changed the subject, it is important to follow her, to stay with her.*)

KAREN. My friend was just walking down the street and a dog tried to attack her, and I saved her life.

(*I am listening in three directions. Listening to Karen: this is clearly a story she wanted me to hear. To Lacy: I am suspicious of the "save her life" bit. To the Holy Spirit: "Lacy, stay with her. Listen for the deep truth she is sharing; she is telling you something about herself. Listen for it."*)

LACY. You did?

KAREN. You remember when I got bit by the dog?

(*This was the subject of much prayer in our community.*)

LACY. Yes, I do.

KAREN. Well, my dad said not to show fear. I wasn't afraid. I didn't show fear. Me and my friend Betsy, you know her? (*I shake my head.*)

We were playing outside, and a dog was there and was growling and barking and, you know, showing his teeth like this. (*Shows me her own teeth.*) I went up to the house and told those people, "Your dog is trying to bite us." And they put that dog in the house. I saved her life. I did the right thing.

LACY. Was God with you then?

(*Listening in three ways: I am hearing that she wants me to know that she is very brave. I wonder if this story is connected in some way to her last story. Like everyone else she wants to be known. Try less to figure her out and know her through her stories.*)

KAREN. Well, yes of course. But I was brave. (*Picks up the third stone.*) You know, God walks around with us.

LACY. What is that like?

KAREN. (*Silent for a bit.*) It kinda feels like the rings when you throw rocks in the water.

LACY. Did you feel that way the day when you saved your friend?

KAREN. I feel that way all the time. (*Picks up the second stone again.*) Look, (*flips it upside down*) it looks like a tomb this way. Like the tomb they buried Jesus in.

(*Notice that she makes another shift in topic. I wonder if she changes topics when she feels that her point was heard by me. I wonder if she changes topics when she is able to hear herself as I mirror or reframe what she has said. This is a mystery; I am still learning to trust the process.*)

LACY. Does that make you feel sad? (*My own assumptions seem to have gotten in the way here. I am glad that she feels the freedom to correct me.*)

KAREN. No, happy. He comes back to life. Well, maybe the tomb is sad. Did you know I go to middle school next year?

LACY. Oh, I think I forgot. How do you feel about middle school? (*The family will be moving to another state in a month.*)

KAREN. I'm worried. Because I don't know anyone in there or at that school.

(*Karen talks a bit more about her current school that she has been in since pre-K and about the people she knows and loves there. This is a tender moment. She is not telling old stories of her bravery or test days at school. This is her reality, and she goes deep to share it. I show her the prayer beads and briefly show her how they work. I tell her she can pray silently or aloud. She takes the beads, closes her eyes, and starts to pray aloud.*)

KAREN. Jesus, I am worried about moving. (*Moves a bead from one end of the string to the other.*) I want us to have a safe trip (*moves a bead*), and I want the car to make it (*moves a bead*). I want my grandpa not to die until we get there (*moves a bead*). Oh, and I'm worried about middle school. (*Moves a bead and says nothing else aloud but slowly and thoughtfully moves each bead until she's at the end. She concludes with a loud pronouncement of "amen."*)

LACY. Before you leave, I'd like to give you a blessing. You can choose the blessing balm or a sweet-smelling cotton ball. (*Karen examines the blessing balm and chooses it. I make a cross on her hand.*) Karen, you are God's child. He loves you, and he is always with you. Thank you, God, for Karen.

KAREN. You better bless my head too. (*Pulls back her bangs.*)

LACY. Okay, I better. (*Makes the cross on Karen's head and repeats the words.*)

Session 2 (two weeks later). Karen is eager to begin. Since it is a lovely spring day after a long winter, I suggest we meet outside. The sun was so bright I didn't think the candle (though fake) would have the same effect outside as it did inside, and since there was a breeze, I knew the picture of Jesus wouldn't stay on the stand. I carry a rosary in my pocket and wondered if it might work instead. I laid the rosary on my Bible and we began.

KAREN. Hey, this is a special spot. (*Points to the white blanket with the green leaves.*)

LACY. Yes, it is. Would you like to join me?

KAREN. Yeah. (*Sits down and immediately picks up the rosary.*) Hey, this is Jesus. And his mom. Um . . . no, Dad.

LACY. It is a rosary, and sometimes I keep it in my pocket to remind me that Jesus is with me. I set it out today to remind us that Jesus is with us.

KAREN. Okay. Can I hold him?

(*I am surprised how interested she is in it and how tenderly she cradles it. I wonder what is drawing her to it. In hindsight, I wish I had asked her.*)

LACY. Sure.

(*Karen holds the rosary gently and occasionally pats Mary's hair. I pray our opening prayer and invite her to choose three stones.*)

KAREN. I'm going to tell you how my day is. (*Chooses a heart, an exclamation point, and a sunshine. Then holds up the heart. Lays the rosary next to the heart stone.*) This is for Lacy. I'm happy to be with you. I like teachers who stay with you.

LACY. Thank you, Karen. Those are very kind words. Can you tell me about the teachers who stay with you?

KAREN. My teacher at school will sometimes stay with me. When I have to stay inside and do my work, she will sometimes stay with me. She is nice.

(*I sense the sacredness of the moment and want to savor it longer than Karen does. She has just offered me a glimpse of her deep longing to connect. She picks up the second rock and shows it to me, then lays the rosary by the second stone.*)

KAREN. This is because I'm excited about camp. My class goes on Thursday. We get to ride horses and four-wheelers. And there's a zip line. I don't know if I want to do that.

LACY. You don't know if you want to do the zip line?

KAREN. It may be too scary. (*Shows me the sunshine stone, and then lays the rosary by the second stone.*) This is how I feel about today. I don't like the cold and the snow. (*It was snowing all last week, but today is sunny.*) Today is sunny. God makes us warm.

LACY. How does God make us warm?

KAREN. Well, he made the sun, didn't he?

LACY. Well, yes, he did.

(*We both laugh and turn our faces to the sun. After a few seconds, she reaches for the rock box and pulls out a few more. She puts the rosary in her lap.*)

KAREN. (*Pulls out the rock with the question mark, and then lays the rosary next to this stone.*) This is how I feel about the move. I don't know.

LACY. You don't know?

KAREN. There's some good and bad, but they'll all turn good. But they're bad right now.

LACY. What's good and bad?

KAREN. The things I told you before. Middle school. My friends are here. But we can swim. You know, those things.

LACY. Oh, anything else?

KAREN. No, just those. (*Pulls out another stone that looks like a foot. She doesn't put the rosary next to this stone, but I think she just forgets.*) This stone is for the church there. They have footsteps on the ground all the way to the children's church room. We visited there. There are lots of kids and prizes. My brother says it's much better than here.

LACY. Do you think so?

KAREN. Yeah. Prizes. (*Pulls out another rock. This one is a cloud; she moves the rosary next to this stone.*) This is like the "Our Father in Heaven" talk. You know where he gives us all we need. Like the cloud gives rain and shade. What we need.

(*As she is going through all the rocks in the box, I wonder if she is using them to externally process the impending move.*)

KAREN. (*Pulls out another rock. This one is a circle with a line through it.*) This is when you break the deal. (*Tells about an argument she had at school today; her friend said she would take the bottom bunk at camp*

52

but changed her mind.) She didn't keep her word. She didn't keep her promise. I don't want friends that don't keep their promises. It's the right thing to do. To keep your word.

LACY. How did that make you feel?

KAREN. Sad. I don't want a friend like that. I changed partners. (*Picks up the rosary and looks at the front and back of Jesus. Pats Mary's hair, again. I wonder what about Mary is speaking to Karen.*)

LACY. (*Holding out a wool finger labyrinth.*) Would you like to use the finger labyrinth to talk with God? It's a tool to help us pray. We talk to God as we move our finger into the center of the circle and then listen to what God has to say to us on the way out.

KAREN. Oh, cool. It's like a maze.

LACY. Yes, it is, a bit. You can use it to pray. You can also use the prayer beads or the paper and markers to pray while drawing.

KAREN. I want to use this. (*Chooses the labyrinth and places the rosary next to it.*) God, help me at camp. And thank you for the sun. And help our move to be good and not bad. (*Gets to the middle and looks at me.*)

LACY. Now you can move out of the labyrinth and listen and see what God has to say to you.

KAREN. (*Looks down and moves her fingers.*) Amen. (*Looks up, grinning.*)

LACY. You can share what God told you, or you can keep it private.

KAREN. Oh, well, this is private.

Session 3 (two weeks later). On this day Karen was very excited. It was her last day of school, and she was given a party and lots of awards. During our last visit she connected with the rosary. I brought it again this time rather than the Jesus pictures and the battery-powered candle.

KAREN. I know just the rocks I want. (*Digs in the box until she finds a footprint, a cross, and a heart.*) This is Jesus walking with me. Even when I walk to the new town. No, we're driving. (*I join her in laughing at her joke.*) The cross is, you know, Jesus died on the cross for me. (*Switches the heart stone for the question-mark stone.*) This one instead. (*Lays the rock beside the rosary.*) I'm worried.

LACY. What are you worried about?

KAREN. The big move. Because we need a house, and they cost a lot of money, but, um, how much do they cost?

LACY. Different houses cost different amounts of money.

KAREN. But we can live with Grandpa for a while.

LACY. What do you think about that?

(*Karen shrugs her shoulders and her eyes fill with tears. She doesn't say anything, and I don't say anything for a few moments. She is running her fingers along the rosary and patting Mary. I am praying for her. My heart is sad too. I can hear the burden she bears; I know I won't see her again. I wonder what I can give her that will sustain her now and in the future.*)

LACY. Would you like to talk to God about this?

KAREN. Uh-huh. I want to use the finger prayer.

LACY. The labyrinth?

KAREN. Yeah, that. (*Points. Takes the labyrinth and lays it gently before her. Then she places the rosary at the center of the labyrinth. She places her finger at the beginning. As her finger moves, she says a few things under her breath that I can't hear. When she gets to the center, she looks up at me, and I see that she has let her tears fall.*)

LACY. Now you can listen and hear what God has to say back to you.

KAREN. (*Smiles and looks back at the labyrinth, weaving her finger out of the center and into the open.*) Amen.

LACY. Did you hear God talk back to you?

KAREN. Uh-huh. God said that we will keep walking.

(*We engage in our usual closing ritual. She asks if she can have a blessing ball and blessing balm. I say yes and bless her.*)

In these few sessions with Karen the rhythm to recognize and respond is woven throughout. Karen used various conversational tools to both recognize God's invitation in her life and to respond to the God who was drawing her. The moments with the most vulnerability and authenticity were when I, as an adult listener, held a contemplative posture, asking only those questions that led to connection with God. Of course, this kind of sight is hindsight, but perhaps we can learn from it.

PROTECTION

While it is of utmost importance that the shift of power during spiritual conversations with children shifts to more freedom for the child, there is one final *P*, one important use of power—*protection*. The inherent power the adult holds should always be used to protect the child. We protect their confidences. The adult listener submits to the God-given autonomy of the child when she keeps their confidences.

These conversations are sacred and are not to be shared with others without the child's permission. Adults enjoy the stories of children, and their ways are an inspiration and a novelty to us, but these stories are not ours to tell. More times than I can count I have seen the flash of anger and shaken trust of children when their parents and teachers tell their stories without their permission.

That said, it is important to remind children and parents that there are times when a confidence must be broken. If a child has been harmed, is in danger, or is a danger to their self or others, the adult listener must break the confidence and report to the proper authorities. In a formal spiritual listening relationship, it can be helpful at the outset to have parents read a statement and sign a release confirming that confidentiality is kept as well as acknowledging when it must be broken.[6]

SOAKING IT IN

The following are suggested topics for conversation with God, with others, or even with yourself.

- Engage these power passages with your imagination: Matthew 18:1-5; 20:20-28; Luke 9:46-48; 22:24-30.

  ▷ Take two minutes before reading a passage and center your heart, mind, and body. Invite the Holy Spirit to speak to you through your imagination. Allow your imagination to serve the Scriptures.

  ▷ Read through the passage once; get the general picture of the passage. Who is present, where is it occurring, what is happening?

▷ Read the passage again, this time pausing to imagine that you are present. Where are you? Who are you? What do you see? What do you smell? What do you hear? What do you taste? What do you touch? Stay in the passage as long as you are able. Let the Holy Spirit guide you in and through this passage.

▷ What does the Spirit want you to know or experience? "Listen with the ear of your heart" (St. Benedict).

▷ Write your response.

- Many of us are not consciously aware of patterns of power. We have lived with them and in them for so long we no longer see them. Begin to notice the patterns of power that surround you. When observing or engaging a conflict, notice the movement of power in the space. When speaking to or about children or differently abled persons, notice how power is being used. Prayerfully hold these observations with the Spirit.

- Reflect on your recent spiritual experience or prayer time. Notice which dimensions of the person were engaged: mind (thoughts and feelings), body, spirit (will), social context (community). Enter into a conversation with God about what might help you to become aware of and engage with your less-dominant dimensions.

four

THE GIFT OF EYES
AND EARS

*To listen another's soul into a condition of disclosure and discovery
may be almost the greatest service that any human
being ever performs for another.*

DOUGLAS STEERE

JUST WHEN I THOUGHT I had become a good listening partner
with my children, they became adolescents and I found myself
again at the beginning. One Tuesday afternoon, my struggle came
to the forefront when my fourteen-year-old daughter and I were
having a bit of vigorous fellowship. She was making her case. And I
was making mine, in my mind, while she was speaking. After part
two of her argument she snapped her fingers and said, "I am right
here. You are not listening." First, my lizard brain kicked in and I
thought, *Did she just snap her fingers at me?* Then the whisper of
the Spirit helped me tune in. Ouch! She was right. I wasn't
present; I wasn't listening. My body was there, but my mind was
in the courtroom preparing my final arguments. Whatever ping

that was possible in our exchange had been missed because I wasn't present and listening. Whatever bid for connection God was extending to us both, I couldn't hear. I missed the possibility to participate in the gift of listening.

In Matthew 18:15-20, when Jesus is teaching about how to have hard conversations, he reminds us, "where two or three are gathered in my name, I am there among them." When we bring our full attention and intention to the child or teen before us, when we open ourselves to another, we also open ourselves to the presence of God. When we are fully present to another, we realize that C. S. Lewis's words in his sermon "The Weight of Glory" are true, "There are no ordinary people. You have never talked to a mere mortal."[1] He reminds us that if we were to see each other as we really are, as God sees us, we would be strongly tempted to bow down and worship one another. When we are fully present to another, we glimpse the imago Dei, the image of God, and it opens us to hear the ping of God.

Being fully present to a child or teen will cost us something though. When we listen with our whole hearts to children, change is the price we will pay—it is the byproduct of vulnerability. For example, I needed to leave the courtroom and suspend my judgment in order to be present to my daughter. I had to risk my own position in order to engage with her. When I moved from her presence to the practical outcome of the vigorous fellowship, I did not hear her longing to be heard or her desire to connect. In order to move back to her, I had to lay my position into the generous hands of the Spirit.

THE GIFT OF EARS

When we are fully present to another, we are listening for longing. As Quaker Douglas Steere puts it, we are listening for "the deepest thing that is already there."[2] The foundation of listening is invitation. At the beginning of all things the Holy Listener whispered and wove a primary cosmic invitation into all creation. This holy invitation is a bid to connect with Love's Family, and it is the place from which profound human-with-human listening flows. Listening is not only a function of the ears but also tuning the heart to the whispers and weaving of God.

Invitation can also take the form of questions that originate in the heart of a person who is curious about the movement of the divine in the life of another. However, curiosity without compassion is merely sterile information gathering, but curiosity laced with empathy and love guided by the Spirit has the potential to listen a child into recognizing their own voice and the voice of God in their life.

Listening isn't all words. Whole-self listening is about being fully present to another. When we are listening with our whole selves to children, we are open in expectation of the wonder of the child's life. In the body, whole-self listening looks like a still and attentive body and active verbal involvement in the sharing.

Whole-self listening is a process that begins with being fully present to God. There are physical steps that help us to be fully present to God. Those steps can look like lighting a candle, which reminds us that God is near. We can also hold an image of God in our mind that speaks to us, or we can pray a simple prayer like, "Help me to be a good listener." Next, we become fully present to ourselves by becoming aware of our breathing, our bodies, our thoughts, and our feelings. Becoming fully present to a child requires both our awareness of God's presence and our awareness of self.

Only after becoming aware of ourselves can we gladly set our *judgmental* self and *good advice* self aside to listen openheartedly to the child. Then, we are poised to be fully present; we are ready to receive the gift of another. And in case you didn't know, children can spot and will name when adults show up to listen but are not fully present. They know what whole-self listening feels like in their bodies. Whole-self listening is the currency of connection, and children are wired for it.

THE GIFT OF EYES

In my early college days I had the incredible opportunity to participate in short-term work in Kazakhstan. On my first trip there I was a part of a team of students who entertained and played with children in a cancer hospital. My deep desire was to introduce these hurting children to the love and friendship I had experienced in Jesus. I watched with my own eyes as their bodies deteriorated, and I longed to draw near to them and their parents. Even at nineteen I knew the deep and inconsolable sorrow of their parents. My own sister, Charity Day, died when she was a baby; I had touched this pain before in the hearts of my parents. These beloveds of God spoke mostly Russian and some spoke Kazakh, but none spoke English and certainly not Texan. How could we connect? How could we listen to one another?

As it turns out, words are certainly helpful in communication, but they aren't a necessity. Much is communicated through our bodies, our unspoken openness, warmth, generosity, and hospitality toward one another. I spent hours sitting at the bedside of Victor, a boy of ten who had a tumor the size of a grapefruit on his neck. I brought the rare gift of oranges and candy, and he gifted me with toys, an octopus and a dog crafted from IV tubing. We had no common tongue for verbal communication, but we did communicate. While playing on the floor and making paper crafts together, I glimpsed his pain, I heard his fear, I sensed his longing, and it is both my hope and my conviction that he sensed the love of Jesus.

All spiritual companions, but especially spiritual companions with children, must not only have ears to hear but eyes to see. We see what is not spoken and feel what is too deep to be articulated. The Holy Listener mediates our listening and clues us into what isn't being spoken but is being said. Victor didn't have to tell me he was disappointed and angry as the other children played outside and he was confined to a small cot in a room full of other sick children. I could sense it in the air around him and joined him there. Together, we tore orange peels into pieces, pulverized them into balls, and threw them at the wall. I wore a small cross around my neck. On several occasions Victor pointed to my cross with a slight smile. I don't know what his exposure might have been to God or the cross, but I hope that my meager attempts at being with him in his sufferings connected him to a God who suffers with him.

In retrospect as a young zealous evangelical, it was probably the very best gospel I could have preached. Surely with the power of words I would have smothered and pressured, maybe even inflicting the same harm inflicted on me as a child. However, without words I was forced to listen, to learn, to watch and read the unspoken language of his heart. And perhaps without my words Victor could truly hear the Holy Listener speak words of comfort and love.

QUESTIONS AS INVITATION

In *The Divine Conspiracy*, in a section titled "The Request as the Heart of Community," Dallas Willard called *asking* the "great law of the spiritual world through which things are accomplished in cooperation with God and yet in harmony with the freedom and worth of every individual."[3] Willard writes that when we offer advice, when we push our pearls upon others, we are their problem, and this keeps them from hearing God or hearing themselves. But when we begin to listen, they do not have to protect themselves from us, and they can begin to open up.[4] This is the power of asking. When we accompany a child in their life with God, asking questions acknowledges the autonomy of the child—the child's ability to perceive, reflect, and respond. Asking open questions also communicates care and curiosity and trust in the child's own knowledge.

Invitation takes the form of "divinely curious" questions. Under guidance from the Spirit the adult is prompted to ask these questions. Divinely curious questions are similar to these: Was there a time in the last week when you knew God was near? or When did you experience something beautiful or good or true? or Can you tell a story about when you felt angry or afraid or happy? The three transcendentals of goodness, truth, and beauty are often the gateway for seeing the action and presence of God and for acknowledging it. When goodness or beauty cannot be recalled, an adult can help a

Figure 4.1. Listening stones are small, smooth river rocks with random symbols printed on them. Through projection, listening stones help children to tell the stories of their lives.

child connect with God through other means, knowing God is present in the child's pain and sorrow, which may be their truth at that moment. As the Spirit is the prompter, questions such as these provide the opening children need to begin to explore and express their inner lives.

Hospital chaplain to children Leanne Hadley created "listening stones" as a way to open up sacred conversation with children.[5] Listening stones are small, smooth river rocks with random symbols printed on them.

Children are invited to rummage through these rocks and choose three rocks that represent the stories of their lives that they want to tell. Additional questions that might invite a child to share are:

What is one thing you are thankful for?

How does a special person or creature in your life make you feel?

A question I have is _____?

Something I want to remember when I grow up is _____?

I wonder about _____?

I feel _____ when _____?

I am thankful for _____?

Something I have trouble with is _____?

Sometimes I feel _____?

When I'm at my best, I am like a _____?

Something I want to remember about today is _____?

Something I am grateful for is _____?

What do you say to God?

What does God say to you?[6]

It's important to remember that these questions are invitations, not tools for an inquisition. Like all invitations, one or two are offered and followed by space in the form of silence and attentiveness. The soul of a child must sense safety and freedom in order to emerge and engage. Silence, attentiveness, and generous openheartedness will communicate that safety and freedom.

For many children, thinking about existential questions is entirely natural and part of what they ponder on a daily basis. These children only need a simple invitation. They welcome the chance to process their thinking and feeling with a listening adult. A helpful question might be something like, Is there anything on your heart you would like to talk about? Psychologist Tobin Hart, who is an expert in children's spirituality, connects the role of the adult and the usefulness of opening questions: "A spiritual friend is especially helpful to offer understanding and guidance, and to pose more questions, 'When have you felt closest to meaning, spirit, God, in your life?' 'When have you felt whole?' 'What do you think life is about?'"[7]

It is important to remember that as children explore their questions, they may confess doubt. When a child expresses doubt it can be unsettling for the adult. However, doubt is part of the ebb and flow of children's spirituality. Children are remarkably free from religious certainty. There is fluidity as they construct and deconstruct their perceptions, understandings, and beliefs. A listening companion to a child can be a faithful witness and a sacred conversation partner as this process takes place.

Once the invitation has been given and children begin to share their inner world, whole-person listening opens up. Listening deeply to children is an exercise in patience and surrender for the adult. Berryman offers us a bit of guidance, "It is worth taking the time to listen and even err on the side of too much listening because the misinterpretation of what a child has attempted to say can be destructive."[8] When adults listen to children, our natural inclination is to try to make the meaning *for* the child. This is decidedly unhelpful due to the fact that we don't have access to all the information or insight into what the Spirit is up to in that particular experience. What a child shares with us is incomplete, it is a glimpse of their life with God, not the whole picture of the experience. If we push our interpretations or good advice onto the child, we may suffocate the child's voice and agency. We may drown out their hearing of God.

The adult must practice the discipline of silence as well as the art of clarifying questions like "Can you say more about that?" or "I'm not sure I understand; can you try explaining it to me?" Questions like these can help to open up the conversation, to allow space for the child to process and hear their own thinking. Children may share a painful or confusing situation, which may trigger our adult urge to fix or save. The adult listener can communicate compassion with phrases such as "I can tell you are hurting/confused/afraid, and I'm sorry."

In allowing space for silence and resisting the urge to fix, adults allow Creator God to interact with God's created being, the child. When these authentic and tender conversations occur, we then create the space for the child to bring their hurt, pain, or confusion to God. Cavalletti says that the most effective role for the adult is one of "mediation . . . a service rendered to the child so that he (or she) may enter into relationship with that source which puts him (or her) in peace."[9]

Not only do we get a partial glimpse of the experience, but children communicate and use language in ways that are unique to childhood. Berryman reminds us that as we listen to children, we hold their words with openness, humility, and wonder.

Entering the world of children is like visiting a strange and wonderful new culture, but the language has a double twist. It sounds like adult language but the words don't always work the same way. Since children have few words and less confidence in them than adults, their words carry more meaning. Their use of language is often more like poetry than prose. In addition their vocabulary is always growing and the usage stays in flux as they continuously experiment with the words they have at their disposal.[10]

Children cannot always put their experiences into words, but they can be quite visual, and young children are certainly more comfortable using pictures to communicate. Stories that children tell follow a cyclical pattern rather than a logic-based linear pattern. Generally, they focus on feelings rather than reason. This is due in part because the right side of the brain develops first. Generally speaking, the right side of the brain is responsible for feelings, creativity, and play. The left side is responsible for reason, language, and certainty. The younger the child, the greater their use of the right side of the brain. Children do not always have the ability to put their thoughts into words. Instead, they communicate in visual images. Therefore, their communication takes the form of circular rather than linear patterns.

This aspect of children makes them more open to wonder, mystery, and union. As Cavalletti explains, "We are dealing with ephemeral moments, like a flash of light that shines vibrantly and then fades away."[11] The role of the adult listener is to recognize the moment too and then create a space for the child to respond. These are the early stages of making meaning, which, when given attention and space, can grow over the course of a lifetime into intimate relationship.

CONTEMPLATIVE LISTENING WITH CHILDREN

Contemplative listening to children does not come natural or easy to adults. Our notions of listening to children have been formed from our own childhood, and therefore it may take some time to relearn a new way of being with children. It may take us time to learn the posture of a listener. Johannes Baptist Metz helps us to get a glimpse of this posture:

> Every genuine human encounter must be inspired by poverty of spirit. We must forget ourselves in order to let the other person approach us. We must be able to open up to the other person, to let that person's distinctive personality unfold— even though it often frightens or repels us. We often keep the other person down, and only see what we want to see; then we never really encounter the mysterious secret of their being, only ourselves.[12]

Can you think of a time when you had the privilege to witness a child's distinctive personality unfold? Contemplative listening with a child means that while we are in "full emotional contact with the child's perceptual experiential world of reality," we maintain a non-anxious centered presence. As play therapist Garry Landreth points out, we "(do) not try to think ahead of the child's experience or analyze the content in some way to derive meaning."[13] Our centered personal presence provides a safe space for children to hear themselves and to hear God.

> If I am to be successful in my efforts to make contact with the child, I must be still within myself and see the child. I must

be still and listen to the child. I must be still and make contact with the imagination of the child. I must be still and follow the lead of the child. I must be still and experience the child. I must be still within myself and touch the hidden inner person of the children. I must be still within myself and wait for the child.[14]

This is easier said than done. When we are listening to a child we may pick up on the emotions of dislike in the child or in ourselves. We may find that we get sleepy or irritated while a child is sharing. How we deal with our own responses determines the amount of freedom a child feels in our presence.

Practice is the only way I know to transform our habits of listening to children. Perhaps you know a few children who might like to be listened to. Ask those children if they would be willing to help you learn to listen. If they are willing, ask for their parents' permission. Then find a twenty-minute block of time and a public spot where you can do some intentional listening. The following guide can help to structure your time.

First, let the child know that you are interested in their life. Communicate that you are here to listen, not to teach or do the talking. Choose one or two of the following questions to ask the child. Notice that many of the questions begin with the word *will*; this important distinction helps to honor the child's agency. This simple word tells children that they are the owners of their stories and further that they can choose to share them or not.

- Will you tell me about a time when you and God did something together?

- Will you tell me about a time when you knew that God was with you?

- Will you tell me a story about something good that happened to you?

- Will you tell me a story of a very strong emotion you had this week? It could be happiness or sadness or anger—anything.

- Will you tell me the story of the most beautiful thing you have ever seen?

- Will you tell me the story of a time when you felt safe or scared?

- I am here to listen, is there something you would like to talk about?

When the child speaks, pay attention to:

- The child's body language. What are they saying without saying?

- How they use words; they may have a different vocabulary for what they are experiencing.

- Their feelings and the meanings they make of them.

- When they are silent. Hold that silence open for them without filling it with your words or actions.

- When your mind starts to drift. It is difficult to pay attention to another for an extended period of time. When your mind starts to drift, notice what is happening in your body.

- Your own responses of anger, sadness, impatience, judgment, or surprise.

When to speak:

- Before speaking take a deep breath and pause. This will help you to speak from the heart and not your head. It will help you to check your responses with the Spirit.

- To help a child continue exploring, repeat the words that seem to be important to the child back to the child.

- Call attention to the presence and activity of God in their experiences.

  ▷ Use "I wonder" phrases such as, I wonder what God is saying to you in this?

  ▷ Continue opening the space for the child to share ask questions such as, Can you say more about that? When did you feel that way before? I don't think I understand, can you help me?

There is a temptation to teach children, and children have been trained to gladly give us the floor, so be aware of this urge and keep your responses short.

- Ask the child if you can pray a blessing prayer when you are finished. Keep it short. For example. Thank you, God, for _____. I am grateful that _____ shared his/her stories with me. Remind _____ that you love him/her very much and that you are always near. Amen.

- For a child who is not familiar with God language: Thank you for sharing your story with me. I am grateful for your life. Love is always near to you.

As we use the gift of ears and eyes with children, we are invited to pay attention to the Spirit whispering at all times.[15] In blessing children we are invited to lend our voice to the Spirit, saying, "I see you. I hear you. I am near to you." In listening and in speaking, we have the sacred opportunity to participate in a child's increased receptivity to the divine invitation for relationship.

SOAKING IT IN

The following are suggested topics for conversation with God, with others, or even with yourself.

- Reflect on the platitude "Children should be seen and not heard." Notice your own response to it. As a child, can you think of a time when that was communicated to you explicitly or implicitly? As completely as you can, tell that memory to God and to your spiritual director or a caring friend. Wonder with that friend how this phrase shaped your own sense of voice and acceptance.

- Conversely, has there been a time when you communicated that message either explicitly or implicitly to children? Be as gentle as you can be with yourself; we do as we've been taught. After spending some time in prayer with the gentle Healer, perhaps you need to seek the forgiveness of a child.

- After sitting with a child in contemplative listening, sit in silence for five minutes. In that silence notice what image comes to mind and heart. Draw that image. Continue to gather images from your sessions, notice what these images have in common, and notice their differences. Are there any invitations emerging from these images?

- Invite the Holy Spirit to alert you when a child makes a bid for connection. It could be at the store with a child you don't know; it could be someone within your family or church. When you notice this bid, make a quick mental check. Use the acronym BOW to guide your check. *B*: Is my body reflecting welcome and the desire to connect. *O*: Am I open to vulnerability and the possibility of change? *W*: Can I wonder with this child about the deepest thing that is stirring in them? To be fully present to a child is to BOW in submission to the One who is present in every encounter.

five

THE LANGUAGE OF PLAY
AND PROJECTION

Birds fly, fish swim, and children play.

GARRY LANDRETH

IN MARK 8:22-26 WE CATCH A GLIMPSE of a playful Jesus. When a blind man asks for healing, Jesus leads him out of the village—where presumably there were fewer spectators—and then as John records it, proceeds to make mud with his own spit (John 9:6). There is something childlike and playful about Jesus healing a blind man with mud made from his own spit. Perhaps Jesus tapped into his own childhood self for this miracle. But things get even more playful when at first it seems the mud does not completely resolve the problem. The man sees something "like trees" walking. The lack of efficiency found in two tries and the willingness to test the process are elements found in play. Lightness, freedom, vulnerability, and healing flow from play. Jesus seems to have known that and like his Father has an infinite capacity for play.

Play is the mother tongue of children. Adults communicate through verbalization, but children who are new to words communicate through play and movement. Play is an essential part of having spiritual conversations with children. It is the primary communication medium. In play children use toys or objects to express, engage, and work out their inner life. Play provides a "symbolic language of self-expression" that can offer us clues to what the child has experienced.[1] During play, children reflect on and make meaning of their experiences, and they resolve the questions that have been stirred up by those experiences. Play allows a child a measure of control in a life governed by adults and can help children feel more secure and safe. Play is more of a process and less of an outcome, which in itself is a freedom and a characteristic of spiritual conversations. And we can be sure that since play is the primary mode of communication for children, God speaks the language of play.

PLAY AND PROJECTION: TOOLS FOR KNOWING

Play and projection are tools for knowing God and knowing self when listening to God with children. Play can incorporate wonder and mystery as well as create the conditions for union. Here's an example of spiritual conversations with a child while playing out the scene of the good Shepherd with wooden objects depicting the story. The adult first tells the story of the good Shepherd, according to a childlike version of Psalm 23, using wooden objects. Then the adult invites the child to play the story.[2] The framework of "playing the story" is the story itself, simply told by the adult. The child is then invited to retell that story and to fill in the framework with their own variations, imaginations, and knowledge.

For example, I have witnessed several children move the shepherd to tame the lion, who represents the enemy wanting to harm the sheep in Psalm 23. The shepherd taming the lion is not part of the biblical story in this passage, but it does represent the deeper longing children have for peace and harmony. I have also seen children move the lion to kill everyone, the shepherd and the sheep. The killer lion is certainly not part of the biblical story either. Here we get a glimpse of the aggression, anger, and frustration that the child feels. The adult listens and watches for the movement of the Spirit as the child plays. Sometimes the Spirit will prompt a divinely curious question, "I wonder why the lion is attacking the sheep?" or reflect back, "I see that the lion is angry."

Sometimes the child will invite the adult into the play, "You be the shepherd" or "You be the lion." As the guest in the play, the adult allows the child to direct. Adults do not step in and reroute, direct, or correct the play in any way. We rest in the unwavering reality that the Spirit is attending whatever is happening within the child. For the child, God is their play partner.

Keeping Catherine Garvey's five criteria of play in mind can help us to notice when a child has moved into play and remind us to surrender our need to problem solve or direct the play.

1. Play is pleasurable.

2. Play is done for itself.

3. Play is voluntary.

4. Play involves deep concentration.

5. Play has links to the creative process, problem solving, the learning of languages and social roles.[3]

Whatever toys or other materials used need to be carefully chosen. The toys must be both engaging and boring enough that a story can be projected on them. For example, video games are engaging, but they are not boring or blank enough to be used in spiritual conversations with children. Toys need to be able to facilitate creative, emotional, and experiential expression. Perhaps it goes without saying, but toys also need to be organized and well kept. A space full of broken electronic toys will distract rather than engage. The aim is to open the space for the child to be heard in the language most natural to them. The aim is not to entertain or placate the child. Play and entertainment are not the same. Interesting enough entertainment does not generally draw us into connection and self-revelation. Play, however, channels the connective energy of experience and exploration.

The following is a list of toys and other materials that are in my listening with children kit.

battery-powered candle

markers, watercolors, watercolor paper

good Shepherd wooden figures

wooden figures that tell stories of Jesus

Silly Putty or clay

emoji balls (faces with emotions on them)

LEGO blocks

laminated Jesus and children images

shallow plastic box with sand

small bottle of bubbles

prayer beads

finger labyrinth

blank blocks

Jenga

SPIRITUAL CONVERSATIONS WITH JAX

On many Wednesday afternoons I can be found at Haven House sitting one-with-one as a listening companion to children. We call this listening time "holy listening," which is a spiritual direction within children's ministry. A listening session can last from fifteen to forty-five minutes, depending on the desire of the child and the flow of the Spirit. We meet together in the playroom, where a spot in the middle has been cleared of broken plastic toys and marked sacred with a white fleece blanket dotted with green leaves. In order to honor the safety of the child, the solid wooden door has been replaced with a homemade canvas door that has a clear, plastic vinyl window. This allows us the safety and privacy we need.

Jax and I met in this space over the course of several listening sessions. As you enter into these recollected sessions with us, notice how play and projection functioned to enable this child to connect with God. Jax is a nine-year-old boy who keeps his distance and very rarely communicates using words. Knowing that play is an essential part of my time with him, I brought a green bag filled with blocks.

Session 1

LACY. Hi, Jax. It is good to see you. (*I sit on the blanket, but he doesn't. He kneels just outside of the edges.*) Would you like to turn on the candle?

JAX. What's in here? (*Grabs the green bag with blocks.*)

LACY. Would you like to play with these? (*Takes them out one at a time and begins to construct what looks like a building.*) Can you tell me about a happy thing that has happened to you?

JAX. The policeman made me happy. He had blue clothes and a black belt. He protects us. His car has loud, loud lights and a gun and a radio. His car is like Batman. It's fast and goes like this. (*Takes a block and zooms it around like a car.*)

JAX. He doesn't shoot people with his gun. He talks on his radio. (*Continues to build in silence for a few minutes.*) At the summer place with the Boys and Girls Club with Amy.

LACY. At the summer place with the Boys and Girls Club with Amy?

JAX. (*Looks in my direction, but not into my eyes, and nods.*) He helps people when they are scared.

LACY. When they are scared.

(*Jax tries to make a building with windows but can't get the blocks to stay on the top of the windows. He puts a block in my hand, and we spend the next few minutes working on the windows in silence together.*)

LACY. Can you tell a story about a time when you were scared?

JAX. That's windows. Praying is like windows. (*Bends down and looks through the windows.*) Look in here.

LACY. (*Bends down, and our eyes connect very briefly through the window.*)

JAX. Like that. You can look and look back. You can ask for help if you're scared.

LACY. When you look, who looks back?

JAX. God does. (*Plays a bit more with the window, peeking at me and me peeking at him.*) I'm ready. (*Takes the prayer beads and begins to move each bead one at a time toward the cross. Still sitting just at the edge of the blanket, he closes his eyes but says nothing. When he is done, he lays the beads down.*)

LACY. Would you like a blessing?

JAX. This. (*Chooses the blessing balm.*)

(*I am surprised. For the last few weeks he chose the cotton ball with the essential oil. I take his hand and draw a simple cross on the back.*)

LACY. God is with you, Jax. And God will never leave you.

Session 2. On this day the pictures of Jesus were the focus of Jax's attention. Jax peeks into the holy listening room as I am setting up, and I ask him if he would like to meet. He says, "Yes, but I don't want to talk very much." I reassure him that he does not have to talk in holy listening. "I'm tired," he says. I nod my head in understanding and sit on the blanket and open a box of cookies. Children are often hungry when they come to holy listening at Haven House. They have just come from school and generally a long bus ride. I have found that having a snack is a small kindness that speaks of hospitality.

LACY. Would you like a cookie?

(*Jax takes a cookie but doesn't join me on the blanket. He is less engaging than he has been in the past. Indeed, he does look tired.*)

LACY. Where have you been today that has made you so tired?

(*Jax lays his cookie down on the floor. At first he doesn't answer my question. He begins to rifle through images of Jesus from* The Jesus Storybook Bible. *He picks up a picture of Jesus and a boy.*)

LACY. What do you think about this picture?

JAX. It's Jesus. This is a boy, and these people are looking . . . and there is a fish and something. (*Lays that picture down and picks up the one behind it.*)

LACY. What do you think about this picture?

JAX. It's Jesus. And a girl and some flowers. She wants those flowers.

LACY. Ah, I can see that. She wants those flowers.

JAX. Love and kindness in them both. Both have some love and some kindness. See? (*Points to the smile on Jesus' face.*)

(*I am surprised to hear him use the words* love *and* kindness. *I wonder what assumptions I'm working with in my own heart that cause the surprise.*)

JAX. I'm done with these. (*Places the pictures back where he found them.*)

LACY. What other story would you like to tell today?

JAX. I went to counseling for my appointment. So much talking. And then I went shopping with my dad and his girlfriend, Sara. I got a toy. (*Reaches behind himself and shows me a toy he brought in.*)

LACY. What was the best part of your day?

JAX. Not the toy. Being with my dad and even Sara. I am tired of talking.

LACY. (*Realizing that I have been asking him questions that require him to talk and remembering that he didn't want to talk, I try to think of something that doesn't require talking.*) Would you like to play with bubbles?

JAX. (*Face lights up and a bit of the tiredness seems to recede briefly.*) Uh-huh.

LACY. Bubbles can be a way to pray without words. You can feel your prayers to God and then blow them through the bubbles. You can blow out the things you are worried about, things that make you sad. You can blow to God the things you need for him to help you with. You can blow your "thank you" to God. It's like talking to God without talking.

JAX. (*Takes the bottle of bubbles enthusiastically then he blows once and stops.*) Catch my prayers. Like this. (*Holds open his hands as an example.*)

(*For the next ten to fifteen minutes I sit on the blanket, Jax is just off the edge, and I hold my hands out catching his bubbles. We don't speak many words. But we laugh and delight in the shapes and colors, with prayers such as "Wow" and "Beautiful." He is perfectly engaged. I see delight.*)

JAX. I am done praying.

LACY. Okay. Would you like a blessing?

JAX. No. Mine is still here. (*Points to his hand. I know he has had all the tactile stimulation he can handle.*)

LACY. I'm glad you told me. May I tell you a blessing?

JAX. (*Nods his head.*)

LACY. Jax, God loves you very much. God is always with you, and God will never leave you.

Reflecting on the session I noticed that sometimes I compulsively search for those "God connections" and want to call them out. But Jax had little capacity for it. When I first suggested the bubbles I expected it to last five minutes. Instead, his praying was almost fifteen minutes. Around the five-minute mark, I told myself I had to lean in and play. I needed to intentionally lose track of time and play in order to stay present with Jax. Playing and praying are similar. Jax invited me to play, "to catch his prayers," and it felt like prayer in my body. Praying past superficiality is often beyond words, and I suspect meaningful prayer is at home in play.

Session 3. When Jax came in, he was wound up. His posture was aggressive, and he was eager to begin. As is normal, he kept his distance and knelt on the edge of the blanket. We started in the same way, and Jax chose five stones, but instead of telling a story for each stone he told one big story for all of them. He chose a heart, a broken heart, a stone with two dots like eyes and a squiggly line like an anxious mouth, an X, and finally one shaped like a tear. Jax began by telling the stories of his holy listening stones.

JAX. I was happy.

LACY. Why is that?

JAX. Because we are here, and it's a good place to be at. But then there was this. (*Points to the broken heart.*)

LACY. What is this?

JAX. A broken heart.

LACY. Um, a broken heart.

JAX. Because they make me read. I don't want to read. I can read. But I don't want to. And then I'm this. (*Points to the face on the rock.*) Then it was this. (*Points to the X.*)

LACY. Can you tell me about this face?

JAX. Mad, but then I was this. (*Points to the tear.*)

LACY. Is this sad?

JAX. Yes. But it turns to this. (*Flips the tear upside down.*)

LACY. Would you help me understand?

JAX. A rain. Rain is good because it waters things. I like to stay here. It is a good place to be at. I don't want to go. Here is a good place.

LACY. Do you mean Haven House? (*Nods his head.*) Where do you not want to go?

JAX. (*Looks at the stone and is silent for a few moments.*) Nothing. I don't want to talk anymore.

(*Something is clearly troubling Jax, but unless he wants to talk more about it, I will let it go. It is not my place to push. Spiritual conversations happen at the elbow. I know that the Spirit can go where I cannot. Upon reflection, I can see that he did speak his fear in his own way. While I may struggle to understand, the Spirit hears every nuance.*)

LACY. Would you like to try something new today? (*Jax nods.*) I have this (*a wooden set of good Shepherd toys and a felt sheet that looks like a grassy area as well as a blue felt pond*). Would you like to play with these while I tell a story about them?

JAX. Okay. (*Slowly sets each piece in place with the water in the front and grass at the back. Places the lion with the sheep. After they are set up, he stops and looks at me, presumably to tell him what to do.*)

LACY. You can keep playing with them if you want to. They are to play with any way you'd like.

JAX. Okay.

(*I read the childlike version of Psalm 23 twice. Jax plays with the pieces, but without any sound. He makes no noises, he tells me nothing, explicitly. It's as if I'm not present. There is no big drama being played out. There are no other pieces involved. The lion is with the sheep and there is*) *no conflict. Jax, who is usually rigid and rarely if ever puts any more than his knees on the blanket, begins to lay on his side. While playing he slowly moves the pieces more and more toward the center of the blanket and more of his body onto the blanket as well. I read the psalm one more time, and by the end only his feet are off the blanket. He is lying on the blanket, quietly playing with the pieces. Neither of us says a word. After a while he asks to pray.*)

LACY. How would you like to pray?

JAX. The bubbles again?

LACY. Sure.

JAX. Catch my prayers again.

LACY. This time would you like to talk to God out loud? (*Probably a little too greedy to hear his inner conversations.*)

(*Before Jax blows the first bubble, he dramatically whispers in a way I can't understand. I get it. No, he didn't want to pray aloud.*)

LACY. (*While I am catching bubbles.*) When you blow out to God, you can blow something that is making you sad. You can blow something you need from God. You can blow your worries. You can even blow the things that make you mad.

(*Before each blow, Jax takes a deep breath. It's as if the breathing itself is connecting Jax to God. Words are not necessary, breathing is enough.*)

JAX. Can I have a blessing now?

LACY. Sure.

Much is going on inside of Jax that he is unable or unwilling to articulate. However, by the end of our time together Jax is at rest, his whole body on the blanket interacting with the good Shepherd, who himself answered Jax's longing for connection. I am reminded that the hiddenness of a child's inner life is a gift. It keeps nosey but well-meaning adults from gumming up a child's early connections with God. Play is a sacred language for Jax, the language the good Shepherd clearly speaks.

Session 4. We begin as usual, though this time Jax sits completely on the blanket. He tells me he won't be able to stay for long because he has a counseling appointment.

JAX. Can we use Silly Putty this time instead of the rocks?

LACY. Sure. How about sculpting a time when God spoke to you?

JAX. (*Takes his time and begins to sculpt.*) He did today. This morning when I was sleeping and the sun was in the windows, not in the windows, coming in the windows. Like a straight light from up there, in heaven, to in my room, like an arrow. Like this (*shows me his sculpture*). Like this arrow pointing up and down. Light going up and down. And God said, "I love everybody."

(*We pause for a few seconds and take in the story he is telling through the Silly Putty.*)

LACY. How did that make you feel?

JAX. Glad.

LACY. What does glad look like?

JAX. It looks like me.

LACY. Who are the "everybody" God loves?

JAX. Oh yeah, me too.

(Just then someone pops into the room and says that the counselor has arrived to see Jax.)

LACY. Can I give you a blessing before you leave?

Children project their interior life through the objects during play. As a result, their projection is a helpful tool for spiritual conversation in that it exposes a bit of their interior lives to the light of day and the praying presence of a listening adult. Children often project their most pressing emotion or need during play, meaning that the objects they play with and the characteristic of the play mirror their own emotion or need. Children play out their concerns and sorrows, their joys and triumphs. Children also play out their perceptions of God, of self, and of the authority figures in their lives. They often play the same theme over and over again as they work through it. When a child ceases to explore a particular theme in play, the adult listener can assume that the child has found a resolution that satisfies them for the time being. Play allows children to not only get in touch with God, but it allows children to get in touch with their own inner wisdom. When a listening adult is allowed to witness these sacred perceptions and progressions, the room becomes holy ground.

PLAY AND PROJECTION IN PRACTICE

Spiritual conversations with children begin where the child is. When starting a holy listening session with a child, we enter the space together. We take off our shoes and sit on the white blanket. I invite the child to turn on a battery-powered candle and provide a prompt about God being light and goodness. This is where we are physically.

Then an invitation is offered to engage the "Jesus and Me" images. These images, drawn by a dear friend and artist Jeannette Fernandez, depict children in everyday circumstances of life: gaming, reading, playing outside, and school. They also depict some common feelings children have, the loneliness of being left out, fear when adults are fighting, abandonment, and comfort. Within each of these pictures is Jesus, who is depicted in the traditional way, so for many children he is easy to identify. Jesus and the children are shown together in childhood situations as the child expresses emotions such as happiness or sadness, fear or safety, loneliness or joy. Through Jesus, the Trinity becomes concrete for children. As a child rummages through these images, they project the thoughts or feelings that are present to them. A few questions like, "Which of these pictures do you see yourself in?" or "Which of these pictures do you like or makes you happy or sad?" can help open up the conversation. This is where the child is emotionally at that moment. It also affirms that wherever the child is, God is there too.

After a child chooses an image, they place it near the candle. As the child is doing so, they are invited to articulate through speech why they chose that image. Listeners might ask questions such as, "How does this image make you feel?" "What do you like about this picture?" "Where are you in this picture?" or "Would you tell me the story of this picture?" In essence the image helps children speak their intention to ask for what they want. Hart explains, "Intention can also help to open the contemplative eye. So many spiritual traditions advise some form of 'Ask and ye shall receive.' Focusing through asking inwardly is like tuning the radio receiver to whatever station you want to hear."[4] In spiritual conversations with children, projection is a tool that helps adults hear more clearly and tune accordingly.

Many children have experienced sorrow and brokenness first-hand. This one formational element of their lives is poised to alienate them from noticing the movement of God by darkening any glimmer of hope. I have found that playing out the life of Jesus brings comfort and friendship into a child's loneliness.

One Advent the children made this clear to me. We had been playing the Nativity story in our session. With blocks we created a hotel and a barn and then played the story with a wooden baby Jesus, Mary, Joseph, shepherds, and all the animals. The children chose to replay the scene where Mary and Joseph ask if they can stay at the inn but are rejected. This was a moment both poignant and telling, as they projected their own homeless situation onto Mary and Joseph. As one boy said, "I didn't know Jesus was homeless too." At that moment I invited him to talk with Jesus while he played out how it feels to be homeless. He nodded his head, and we were silent for a few minutes while he played and prayed.

We might think that children at Haven House have rare experiences of sorrow and brokenness, but that couldn't be further from the truth. Most children have experienced sorrow, grief, and brokenness; it just isn't as loud as the brokenness at Haven House. For example, Kendal, an eight-year-old girl, played out the story of Jesus healing a child. "The child is me," she said, "when I am old and die like Grandma." Kendal was working out her questions about life and death and sickness and healing, projecting her fears into the play and allowing Jesus to meet those fears. All children need a listening partner to hear whatever is stirring within them.

CREATING AS PLAY

Children also play by creating. Having art materials on hand like watercolor paints and watercolor paper or clay to sculpt can provide another medium for projection. Children who are not familiar with Jesus or who may have different religious traditions not connected to Jesus need not miss out on the gift of a listening adult. Inviting a child to draw or create something that tells the story of their experience of goodness, beauty, or truth encapsulates the benefits of projection and connects the child with their Creator through the act of creation. Children are born creators and will build or shape almost anything to express themselves. LEGO blocks are a wonderful medium for children to create their communication with God.

In any given listening session, playing and creating might look like imagining a story with the characters from *Inside Out*, a Pixar film about feelings, to tell about anger, sadness, joy, fear, or disgust. It might look like playing out one of the stories from the life of Jesus with wooden toys. It might look like playing a game of Jenga while exploring existential questions. Through imagination, play helps children integrate their outer world and their "inner perception of meaning."[5]

SOAKING IT IN

The following are suggested topics for conversation with God, with others, or even with yourself. As a child's conversation with God includes activity, allow these activities to be conversation.

- Locate a place to observe children at play. The nursery at your local house of worship or a preschool are good places to check.

Be sure to obtain permission, explaining that you are seeking to learn to "hear" children while they are playing.

> ▷ As you are observing, notice your own thoughts or feelings. Do some of your own childhood experiences come to mind?

> ▷ Notice one child who captures your attention, and ask the Spirit to help you "hear" what the child is saying through prayer. What longings or desires do you hear? Pray for this child while listening.

- Locate a child who will teach you to play. It may be a family member or a friend of your family. Ask the child to teach you to play. Allow the child to choose the activity and direct you while you play.

> ▷ Notice your resonance and resistance while playing.

> ▷ Notice when you lose track of time.

- What is one thing you liked to do when you were a child? Did you love to dance, ride horses, or paint? Take some time to re-introduce yourself to this play practice.

six

ATTENDING
THE SPIRIT

God's presence can't be spooned out in small and controllable doses.
It comes when and where it will.

JEROME BERRYMAN

FOURTEEN-YEAR-OLD GIRLS DON'T OFTEN begin by sitting on
the floor. Most are not sure if they want to be grown-ups or children.
So, they choose the chairs and then more often than not move to the
floor where the toys are, but only after the space feels safe to them.
When asked if she'd like to sit on the floor or on the chairs, Joanna
surprisingly chose the floor. She dumped out the bag of holy listening stones and began telling the stories of her day using every
stone. There was nothing remarkable about her day. No sharp emotions, no drama, no noticeable acts of kindness, no sorrow or fear.
However, in each story she described there was quiet goodness. At
the end of her sharing, I asked if she would like to ring a meditation
bell and we would listen until the sound was all gone, and then we
would listen even deeper and hear what God may be saying through

the events of her day. She liked the idea and rang the bell, and we settled into listening hearts. "I almost want to cry," Joanna said, slowly breaking our silence after a few minutes, "God loves me, and I'm so happy."

In spiritual conversations with children, listening adults are attending to how the Spirit is moving in the life of a child. The movement of the Spirit can look like quiet goodness in the midst of a normal day in the life of a fourteen-year-old girl. The movement of the Spirit can also look like an awakening to the love of God that moves us to tears.

ATTENDING THE SPIRIT IN THE LIFE OF A CHILD

An adult listener learns to see and hear by becoming a person of prayer. Through consistent prayer practice, the adult has learned to attune their heart and mind to the movement of the Spirit. To be sure, adult listeners never master the art of attunement but are always intentionally learning to attend to the Spirit. Intentional learning implies that we use our will and resources to cultivate a contemplative posture of prayer. If, like me, you have grown up in a tradition that doesn't quite embrace the word *contemplation*, you might be wondering just what that means? Contemplation is a listening posture; it is a way of being that presses our ear to the heart of the divine. Listeners with children learn to listen to the Spirit in the silence of their own heart as well as in the world around them, including the world of the child.

The Spirit is active in at least two main ways during a listening session with a child. First, through the Spirit's pervasive presence in the session itself. All of the listening, playing, creating, recognizing, responding is happening through the Spirit and because of the Spirit. The spiritual conversation itself is an experience of God. The Spirit is also active through loving attention to the expansive life of the child. When we create a space where a child can talk about their experience of God, we help to lay down a neurological footprint in the brain that helps the child to identify and therefore experience the Spirit in the future. Human beings have experiences with the Spirit throughout their whole lives. However, without naming and reflecting on those experiences, these experiences can get buried under the comings and goings of everyday human existence.[1]

Noticing the movement of the Spirit in the life of a child requires that the listening adult release a measure of control and expectation. Adult listeners know God is present and enter into a listening session with the expectation that God will speak. Eastern Orthodox priest John Oliver reminds us, "We affirm that not only does everything that has being have God as its source but also that, because God is good, everything is fundamentally good."[2] Tuning in to fundamental goodness involves listening for experiences of beauty, goodness, and truth. It also involves listening for moments of authenticity that have the character of tenderness. Authentic moments also flow from the presence of sorrow or pain. The Spirit meets the child in each of these experiences and offers comfort exhibited as centered confidence in God and self or as compassion for friends and gentleness with siblings.

Adult listeners also help children tune into the deep peace of God. This peace is not "a superficial sense of pleasure or feeling good or merely being happy. . . . (I)t is a profound sense of well-being and aliveness" that flows from resting in God's presence.[3] Children have described this sense as "what it feels like when you put in the last puzzle piece," "when you're swinging super high and you know God's there," "when I lie in my mom's lap," "the smell of my grandpa's shirt," "when the kid who doesn't get picked, gets picked," and "when I'm stuck on a math problem and my teacher helps me." When children learn to listen for this peace and name it as evidence of the Spirit, it can help them connect to God in louder times; it can help guide them in life's decisions and offer them hope in seasons of loneliness.

To be sure the Spirit will always work in the life a child that yields "love, joy, peace, patience, kindness, generosity, faithfulness, gentleness, and self-control" (Galatians 5:22-23). We can listen for this fruit and name it when we see it, but we don't aim for the fruit. As friend and pastor Paula Frost says when speaking about children's spirituality, we "water the root, not the fruit." The root is the child's relationship with God, and the watering can is listening.

Attending to the Spirit with children also requires that the adult releases outcomes into the hands of God. It is the Spirit who first whispered love into the child's heart. And the Spirit is ultimately responsible for formation and transformation. Aiming for outcomes such as behavior modification takes the role of the listening adult beyond its natural limitations. Spiritual conversations help children to drink from the streams of living water that are already flowing; the results of the drinking are up to the Spirit.[4]

We must always keep in mind that the mode the Spirit uses to cultivate a relationship with a child is unique to that child, certainly unique to each person. Humans are gloriously diverse in almost every way, and therefore the modes that we engage with the Spirit will be too. Children may experience God by feeling the wind on their face, in their first bike ride alone, in comforting words from an adult, in the purr of a cat, in the random color combinations of a LEGO creation, in the kindness of a fellow student at the pencil sharpener, in the quiet lights on a darkened street, or in the taste of mac and cheese: the list is endless! Each of these in their own way can lead to deeper experience and relationship with God. When the experience is heard and named as a with-God moment, the relationship deepens.

The Spirit also moves in the mode of contrition. The Spirit who formed and knows each child from their very beginning is always calling them back to their truest self. Conviction in the life of a child might feel like unrest, agitation, a haunting knowing that whatever the child is embodying at that moment is just not right. Children can and do feel this disequilibrium of the soul. We do not need to manipulate or pressure children to respond to their contrition. We only need to help make a safe space for children to process what they already feel. Through our posture and presence, we make a safe space, free from judgment, for a child to speak their "I'm sorrys." To be overtly clear, it is not the job of the adult listener to make judgments or to correct. Children have other adults who will do that. The listening role is to embody the hospitality of Jesus, who welcomed the children with open and affirming arms.

MACEY'S CONTRITION

It was an extremely hot day in July at Haven House. Because of the heat and lack of air conditioning, we were having our holy listening sessions outside under an oak tree. With our blanket spread out on the grass, Macey and I entered the cool of the sacred space and sat together. "I don't need the rocks," she announced even before we began, "I know what I gotta talk about." I breathed a prayer asking for help from the Spirit, knowing I was already in over my head. Macey was eleven years old going on twenty-five. She didn't only look mature beyond her years but her experiences were such that no child should ever carry. She was scrappy, resilient, and tough as nails.

Her blue fingernails picked at the edges of our blanket. "You know all the crap I get from my mom. 'Be here at this time. No, you can't do that. Change your clothes.' Blah, blah, blah. And like I get so mad about that because she does it. I'm the one that cooks dinner when she's not home. And I'm the one that makes sure Missy's homework is done. And I just want to say, 'I hate you. I can make my own decisions.' Well, I did. Finally, I said that, and I stole her wallet."

"So, you said what you wanted to say, and you stole her wallet," I repeated back to her, careful to use her words and add none of mine that might lead her to think I was holding court over her wounds. "Yeah, I gave it back a few hours later, and I didn't take anything from it, but I did take it. I feel kinda good and bad about the fight," she said. Again, I mirrored her words back to her, helping her to hear herself, "It feels kinda good and bad." We don't often hear ourselves. We hear what others say, and we hear what we think they are saying. Children especially are rarely given a chance to reflect on what they themselves say, think, or want.

"Good, like what I said is the truth and bad like I don't know why I stole her wallet. It's so stupid." I listened a bit more about what feelings were underneath these wounds, and then I asked, "Would you like to talk with God about the good and the bad using any of our prayer tools?" She did. She used the tray of sand and some sticks she found to scrawl her response in the naturally shifting and temporary medium.

"There. I'm done," she declared with a swoosh of her hand to erase any trace of her confession. Macey had come to holy listening with the conviction from the Spirit that she was not embodying the truest part of her self. She was compelled to respond and receive what immediately follows, comfort and peace. As I drew a Celtic cross on the top of her hand with the blessing balm, she blessed me back by thanking me for listening. "I feel so much better," she said with relief.

ATTENDING MY OWN INTERIOR MOVEMENTS

While paying attention to the movement of the Spirit in the life of the child, the listening adult is also noticing the movement of the Spirit in their own life. It benefits a listening adult to be in an adult listening relationship—like spiritual direction. Spiritual conversations with children can open up childhood wounds and experiences with God. Having a safe and competent conversation partner to help you live into and through your experiences will draw you deeper into life with God as well as help you to be a more available and attentive listener to children. German theologian Karl Rahner skillfully articulates that we bring our childhood selves and our adolescent selves with us into our adult lives.[5] Our experiences of God, our understanding of love, belonging, and authority are pieces of our God experiences even in adulthood.

We do our own inner work for the child we listen with as well as for our own life in God. Thomas N. Hart, theology professor and family counselor, instructs that so much of human learning is through modeling.[6] It is particularly true in spiritual conversations with children. A listening adult is modeling the listening life with God. It is very difficult if not impossible to listen for what we have not heard.

The aim of spiritual conversations with children is not doctrinal knowledge of God. The aim is to keep hot the living, breathing relationship with God that is already happening within the child—whatever that looks like. While listening with children, we attend to the Spirit in the life of the child, we are helping a child learn the fine art of divine perception. But perhaps it's more like Jeffery's description, said one afternoon while painting a picture of the praying mantis he spotted and studied during holy listening, "It's like we're detectives looking for the fingerprints of God."

SOAKING IT IN

The following are suggested topics for conversation with God, with others, or even with yourself.

- Think back to significant moments in your life. Choose one of those moments to hold in conversation with God. Ask the Spirit to show you how and when the love and care of others was of the Spirit's prompting.

- Listening to the Spirit is centered in silence. If we have not learned to keep silent before God, it is unlikely that we will be able to keep silent before a child. Build fifteen to twenty minutes of holding still and silent before God into your day. For me, early morning before my house wakes up is a good time. For you, it might be late at night after your house goes to sleep. In your mind hold a welcoming image of God. Practice releasing the thoughts, feelings, memories, and inclinations into the hands of God. Allow your mind to descend into your heart and just be before God.

- Practice noticing the movement of the Spirit in your everyday life. Begin by asking the Spirit to help you to see the Spirit's movement in the ordinary. Then begin to look for moments of goodness, either received or expressed goodness; look for moments of beauty, a created thing or interaction that expresses goodness through the senses; look for moments of truth, those rare and lovely occasions when something is authentic and vulnerable. After each, offer a short prayer of gratitude.

seven

WHOLE PERSON
PRAYER

*The task of nourishing spirituality is one of releasing, not
constricting, children's understanding and imagination.*

DAVID HAY

CHILDREN ENGAGE THE WORLD with all the dimensions of
their person, and therefore they also engage with God with all the
dimensions of their person. A whole child spiritual experience is
one in which the body, thoughts, feelings, will, spirit, and social
context come in contact with God.

Jacob had been meeting with an adult listener over Skype for two
months. He explained how he experienced God during his tenth
birthday. "I was getting ready to blow the candles out. Mom and
Dad and everyone were singing, and the candles were so bright—it
was kinda orange and blue—and I sucked in to blow them out, like
(he breathed in loudly) and it was like I breathed in God. It was like
happy and together, like a warm hug." Jacob's spiritual experience
included his body (he breathed in), his thoughts and feelings (happy,

together), his will (he wanted to connect with his family and with God), and his social context (his family and friends were conduits of love and care).

DIMENSIONS OF THE CHILD

A child begins life in unity with the dimensions of their self. Therefore, whatever ways we accompany them must include all their dimensions. A child has a mind, where thoughts and feelings reside. A child has a spirit or a heart, which is wired to long for God, and wired for agency. A child has a body that is made to explore the world. And a child has a social context or family and friends, where mutual formation occurs. For example, children may experience wisdom as a bodily feeling, a sense of knowing in much the same way they experience satiety. Wonder and awe are closely tied to the emotional center of children. Children often express wonder and awe through their bodies: wide-open eyes, sudden silence, or insatiable curiosity to experience the object of wonder or awe with touch.

While most adults have split the self in order to negotiate the harsh realities of the world, a child's self remains intact. The younger the child, the more connected the dimensions of the self remain. This means that children experience prayer through each dimension. Children not only *think* or *feel* a prayer with their mind but also are inclined to use their body to pray (for example, using a finger labyrinth). Children might also experience prayer or connection to God through family and friends. For children the lines that differentiate the dimensions blur and do not matter. All is experienced as connection to God. If we want to have fruitful spiritual conversations with children, two actions are required of us.

First, we need to reconnect with the dimensions of our self that as adults we have estranged. We may have become more mind and thought centered and moved away from integration with our bodies. Our encounters with God may have become overly private, leaving out our community or social context. Second, observe children. Notice how they engage the world and God with the various dimensions of their person. Ask a child to teach you to pray as they do. Enable empathy and agency in a child by being vulnerable and sharing a glimpse of a struggle that you currently have. (Be sure that your struggle is appropriate for a child.) The universal experience of being left out is felt by adults and children. Share a bit of your story, and then ask the child if they have ever felt like you do. Notice how God speaks to you through the child, notice how God comes alongside you.

THE CHILD IN PRAYER

Children are invited into the many expressions of Christian prayer. While prayer can be defined as talking with God, with children *talking* can take the form of shared images, shared feelings, or playing. It may be that what a child wants to communicate cannot be put into words; they may be unable, or it may be beyond words. As Berryman reminds us, "An encounter with the mystery of God's presence is ineffable."[1] Artistic expression creates a deep space of connection between God and children. When children apply their imagination and creativity to their inner world, deep feelings or experiences become concrete.

This might take the shape of sculpting their response to God out of Silly Putty or using watercolors to paint how they feel about losing a friend. Connecting prayer with bodily experience heightens children's experience as well. One boy who told the story of how angry he was with his brother stood up, widened his arms and squatted like a gorilla, then prayed, "Watch me, this is how I feel, God!" Telling the truth about how he felt had to be told with his body. Children also like to take deep breaths and connect how they feel with their sense of God's presence. "God is with me; I am safe," is a popular breath prayer among children, and practicing a breath prayer with bubbles can introduce an element of play.

Inviting children to create prayer practices can unleash their imagination for good. During nature walks children often want to stack rocks as their form of prayer. I have also witnessed jumps of joy and small leaf creations as responses to the Spirit. Creating a bodily prayer from the words of the Lord's Prayer is one example.[2] Creating a prayer collage out of magazine clippings can help a child bring what they know about themselves and interweave it with what they know about God, a powerful visualization of the withness Love's Community offers.

In her book on group spiritual direction Alice Fryling advises asking the question, "What would be helpful to you right now?" which is a great question for inviting children to choose a prayer practice.[3] Some children will claim to not know what would be helpful to them. A lifetime of adults telling children what they need has blunted their ability to hear their own longings. A great gift of spiritual conversations with a child can be to help the child hear their own needs, desires, and longings.

We begin by asking what would be helpful, and then if the child says they do not know, we take a step back and begin asking questions around desires. Sometimes a child will want to feel safe or happy or confident. Knowing that longing can help guide what would be most helpful and even how the prayer might take shape. For example, a child who wants to experience peace might be asked, "Which way to connect with God would help you feel peaceful?" Painting a prayer, using the prayer beads, taking a walk, or blowing bubbles might help a child experience the peace of God. Helping a child connect with God and connect in a way that reflects their own desires engages the child's will or agency, an important dimension of the self.

When telling the story about a conflict in middle school, Bethany confessed, "I know I should ask God to help me forgive her." Children who have been raised in church have many advantages, but one major disadvantage is that they aren't used to listening to their own wants. The use of the word *should* revealed that Bethany's desires weren't matching up with what she thought God and adults would want from her. She could hear the wants of others, but what did she want? After a bit more conversation Bethany felt hurt and needed someone to hear her pain and to even feel it alongside her. Her conversation with God began right where she was, with her hurt.

The form of the prayer may vary from child to child and from session to session. Involving various dimensions of the person in the prayer practice helps children to connect with God on a deeper and more lasting level. It can be helpful to widen our understanding of prayer and remember that all conversation has the potential to be prayer. The unseen loving Other is always seeking connection and responding to the child's spoken or unspoken longings.

TOOLS FOR RESPONSE: PRAYER BEADS AND LABYRINTHS

Children are bodily in nature and therefore benefit from prayer tools that engage the various dimensions of their person. (Adults benefit too, but that's another matter.) While prayer tools can be purchased, I invite you to create them yourself. Before the less crafty of you burn this book, let me remind you of the benefit of contemplative, embodied presence. Children pick up on our own life with God, which is communicated through a nonanxious, centered presence. Without words, our very presence communicates the peace and patience of God, but this doesn't happen in an instant. Centered personal presence is the product of time soaking in God's loving gaze. The desert mothers and fathers learned that moving the hands allowed the mind to descend into the heart. In this space they could be attentive to the inner desires of their heart and the movement of the Spirit. Since it worked for them, perhaps it can work for you too.

Take a deep breath, gather your materials, and try creating prayer beads.

Creating prayer beads. Gather your materials: at least twenty-four inches of string or cord for making a bracelet (the length depends on the size and number of beads), cross pendants in several colors, and a package of beads.

Figure 7.1. Creating and using prayer beads can help children to include their bodies in prayer.

Before beginning, center your mind and heart on the presence of God near to you. Take a few deep breaths and greet God. "Welcome, God."

Look at the crosses. Pick up two or three and notice the color and shape. Choose the cross that reflects where you are in your relationship with God today. Remember to be as gentle with yourself as God is with you. Notice where you are without judging where you are. Judging is above your pay grade mainly because we human persons are finite, so we never see the whole picture—even perhaps especially our own picture.

Look at the cord. Run your fingers along the edges; notice the color and texture. Choose the cord that represents your lifelong walk with God. Using a ruler, measure out two feet of cord. Cut your cord. Thread your cord through the hole in your cross and then tie a knot.

Look at the beads and begin to listen to God. Reflect on the following points as you notice the colors, shapes, and textures of the beads.

- Choose a bead that represents an early encounter with God.
- Choose a bead that represents an early encounter with love.
- Choose a bead that represents an early encounter with beauty.
- Choose a bead that represents an early encounter with nature.
- Choose a bead that represents an early encounter with sorrow.
- Choose a bead that represents an early encounter with joy.
- Choose a bead that represents an early encounter with mystery.
- Choose a bead that represents an early encounter with kindness.

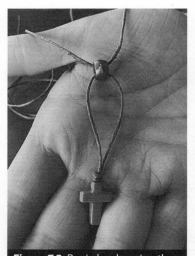

Figure 7.2. Begin by choosing the cross that represents where you are in your relationship with God today.

Figure 7.3. Reflect on your life as you notice the colors, shapes, and textures of the beads.

Figure 7.4. As you string your beads continue to listen to both your inner stirrings and God.

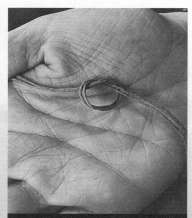

Figure 7.5. As you tie the knot at the very end, offer thanks for the woven cords of meaning threaded throughout your life, knitting you into the Trinitarian Community of Love.

- Choose a bead that represents an early encounter with patience.

- Choose a bead that represents an early encounter with peace.

- Choose a bead that represents an early encounter with wonder.

Gather these beads together in a group. From the group choose five to seven beads.

Consider the order in which you would like to string your beads.

Begin to string your beads while continuing to listen to both your inner stirrings and to God. Figures 7.2 and 7.4 show you how to string your beads.

When you have finished stringing your beads tie a knot at the very end (see fig. 7.5). As you do, offer thanks for the woven chords of meaning threaded throughout your life, knitting you into the trinitarian Community of Love.

This is also a helpful contemplative exercise to do with children. Children at Haven House often ask to create their own set of prayer beads. While the practice of creating the prayer beads is contemplative, it's also a travel-friendly, physical reminder of the ongoing invitation of God.

The contemplative practice of praying using labyrinths. Labyrinths have been around for hundreds of years. People have used them for many reasons, but Christians have been using them for prayer and pilgrimage since the Middle Ages. Labyrinths offer children the opportunity to use their bodies in their prayer life. While you can search for places in the community where a walking labyrinth can be found, it is also possible to make one yourself. A child-sized labyrinth can be created from a king-size bed sheet.

Figure 7.6. Labyrinths offer children the opportunity for prayer and pilgrimage.

Roughly sketch the pattern of figure 7.6 on a white or light-colored bedsheet and then gather a few friends to help you color the pattern with permanent markers (see fig. 7.7).

I have found that children need a bit of instruction to walk a prayer labyrinth. As they begin their walk, their own existential questions rise to the surface with each step and each twist and turn. The slow, intentional walking allows children to reflect on their questions and bring them to God. When an adult listener sets the tone of the time as sacred space to talk with God, children naturally let their bodies lead them into shared conversation.

Offer the child a few simple words of guidance like, "you can talk to God on the way into the center, then take three deep breaths at the

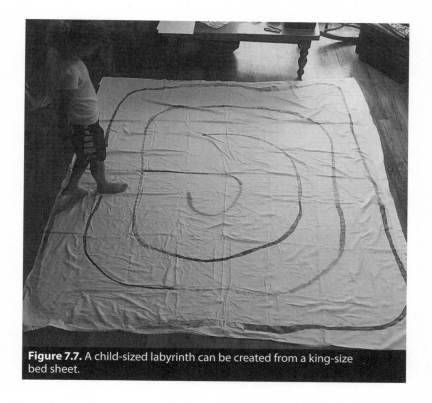

Figure 7.7. A child-sized labyrinth can be created from a king-size bed sheet.

center, and last, listen to God on the way out." For children who can read, a guided prayer page can help them to listen inwardly. See the Three Guided Prayer Pages for Walking a Labyrinth in appendix 2.

Larger labyrinths aren't always practical for travel or for the designated listening space. In that case, finger labyrinths work just as well. A quick internet search of "finger labyrinths" will turn up many options in various sizes and costs. If you are feeling adventurous, my website *Good Dirt Ministries* has a blog post titled "The Contemplative Practice of Felting a Finger Labyrinth" that has instructions on making your own finger labyrinth out of felted wool.[4]

Figure 7.8. Children can create a sacred space to connect with God using all the prayer tools at their disposal.

Children use a finger labyrinth in the same way that they use a walking labyrinth. The easy rhythm of speaking and listening both to their own inner voice and the voice of God frames the intention. Due to the size and portability, children can combine the finger labyrinth with other prayer tools and create a sacred space all their own that reflects their longings, desires, and the responses of love they have sensed.

WHOLE-PERSON PRAYER WITH BRANDAN

Notice the movement and expression of the whole self of the child in the following excerpts from four spiritual conversation sessions with Brandan.

Session 1. Brandan has just completed kindergarten. He is an unusually verbal boy. Due to his age, holy listening lasts twenty to twenty-five minutes. On this day he popped into the holy listening room and asked "Is it my turn? I need some listening," I said "sure" and inquired about permission from his mother. He offered me a sneaking smile and then ran off. When he came back, only minutes later, he was holding a large container of Fruit Loops and the signed release form. Brandan kicked off his shoes and made himself comfortable on the blanket. I began to explain about some of the things we would be using. He listened but was preoccupied with the Fruit Loops. He picked out seven or eight of the blue Fruit Loops and handed them to me. "You like blue," he said. I thanked him and ate them because nothing says acceptance like soggy Fruit Loops. After that he put them aside and began to dig through the bag of holy listening stones.

BRANDAN. These are the ones. (*Chooses a heart, a squiggly line arrow, and an arrow pointing straight down. He then picks up the heart and shows it to me.*) This is for my dad. He died.

LACY. I'm sorry, Brandan. How does the heart remind you of him?

(*Although that is quite a startling story, I want my own feeling response to match the one he has. I do my best, to stay with him where he is and deal with my own response later.*)

BRANDAN. Because I love him, and I miss him. And this was broken when he died. (*Plays with the rock a bit and then lays it down by the battery-powered candle.*)

BRANDAN. This one. See the squiggly line. It's a turning thing. Not supposed to be . . . things that make me sad.

LACY. What else makes you sad?

BRANDAN. School is over. I like school. And my teacher likes me and so do the kids, and we talk and play. We play outside.

LACY. Am I hearing you say that you are sad that school is out?

(*Again, Brandan doesn't say anything. He goes back to the box of Fruit Loops and grabs a handful. I am a little apprehensive that he might offer me some again.*)

LACY. Would you like to talk more about school being out?

BRANDAN. No, I want to talk about this. (*Picks up the next rock.*) See this line pointing down. It's down because God made it. Everything from God comes down here. He draws everything and it's here. I feel happy with this one because he made everything good.

LACY. (*Wondering if he is telling the creation story and where he heard it. I silently give thanks that the God he knows makes everything good.*) What are some of the things that are good?

BRANDAN. My mom and Haven House and toys and you and Fruit Loops and trees and bikes . . . that's all I can think. (*Names several other things he sees in the toy piles and outside of the window.*) I am ready to pray.

BRANDAN. What's this?

LACY. It's a finger labyrinth, like a maze, for praying. What if we do it together first?

BRANDAN. Okay. Good.

LACY. (*I place my index finger at the entrance and begin. Brandan places his finger behind mine and follows. I pray aloud.*) Thank you, God, for Brandan and help him to know that you are always with him. And help him to find something fun to do this summer. Thank you for listening when he said he misses his dad and his teachers and his friends.

(*When we get to the center of the labyrinth, we pause, and I explain that now we listen to what God is saying to us. And then when we finish the labyrinth we can say amen. In silence his finger follows my finger outward.*

I am praying silently as he is praying, asking God to speak just what his tender soul needs to hear.)

LACY. Did God speak to you?

BRANDAN. God said, "I love Brandan." Can we do it again? But you follow me.

LACY. Sure.

BRANDAN. (*This time Brandan leads our prayer time. With our index fingers I follow him through the labyrinth. He prays aloud.*) God, I miss my dad. But I like Haven House and the computers. I love you Jesus, and I want school back. (*Pauses and with his other hand he moves the battery-powered candle to the middle of the labyrinth.*) And the good things. (*Pauses at the center and begins his way out, silently.*)

LACY. Amen. Did you hear God speak to you?

BRANDAN. He said, "I love you too."

Session 2. Brandan was in the holy listening room when I arrived. He was anxious to meet with me. He turned on the TV while I was setting up. He had a cartoon video of two trains "that were friends." He declared that since we were friends, we should watch it together. After some negotiating, we decided that he could watch it while I set up; then we would turn it off during holy listening. If I didn't have another child for holy listening, we would turn it back on and watch it together. My lofty ideals for spiritual conversation were going to be incarnated in friendship whether I liked it or not.

LACY. Brandan, would you like to join me on the blanket, and we can start holy listening?

BRANDAN. Okay. Lemme see this. (*Picks up the picture of Jesus and the children from* The Jesus Storybook Bible. *It has been there each week we have met, but this is the first time he has interacted with it.*) I think it's Jesus.

LACY. Yes, and anyone else?

BRANDAN. A boy. (*There is another picture behind it of a girl with Jesus. Jesus is giving the girl some flowers.*) I like this one better. She is saying, "God loves me." (*Puts the Jesus picture with the boy off the blanket and the picture with the girl on the stand next to the battery-powered candle.*)

(*I offer him the bag of listening stones. Instead of choosing three rocks, he pours all out on the blanket. He carefully arranges them, turning their symbols upward. He pulls out the heart and puts it first. I ask him the same set of questions we have used in the past three weeks, but he won't really engage. I watch as he arranges and sorts the stones. I wonder what he'll do with blocks. I dump a bag of blocks out beside the rocks.*)

BRANDAN. Okay. I'll build something. Maybe a house. (*Begins to build a house with the blocks but struggles to get them to stand up and asks for my help. We build together. Then he picks up the broken heart rock and shows it to me.*) He was always crying and screaming. I didn't want him anyway. (*I wonder who the "him" is but don't want to disrupt what might be happening with God in his heart. He begins to pick up the rocks and tell me who they are.*) This one is me. (*Puts the rock in a little block room he's built. Then he puts the battery-powered candle in the room with the rock that represents himself.*) Jesus is with me.

LACY. What does Jesus say to you?

BRANDAN. He told me my house burned down. But he will build it. (*Says this without looking at me as he works on the roof of the house.*) This is my brother. He's in here with me and Jesus. (*Places his mother at the opposite end of the house; her new boyfriend is with his mom. His grandfather is also in the house, but not in the special room with Jesus. Brandan plays with these blocks and rocks for some time. It's the longest session we've had. After a bit he asks if we can pray and watch the TV together.*)

LACY. How about we try a new way to talk to God today? Would you like to try praying with bubbles?

BRANDAN. Oh! I love bubbles! How do I do it?

LACY. First, think the thing you want to say. Maybe you want to tell God about something fun you did today. Then, blow those words into the bubbles.

BRANDAN. (*Wants me to hold the container, while he handles the wand.*) I like my new video. (*Blows two dips of bubbles.*) And I like these. (*Points at the bubbles and laughs and blows some more.*)

LACY. Now, maybe you want to tell God something that makes you sad.

BRANDAN. (*Pauses but says nothing. Instead, he blows and blows. He spends the next few moments trying to get the bubbles to land on the roof of the room where he and Jesus are. When he does, there is jubilant celebration.*)

BRANDAN. Shouldn't I have a blessing?

LACY. Yes, you should. Would you like blessing balm?

BRANDAN. The one on my hand.

Session 3. Brandan is waiting for me when I walk in the door. I tell him I need to set up and he can help me. While he's helping me, he mentions getting in trouble at the Boys and Girls Club. When the room is set up, he leaves and comes back with a tub of cereal of some sort. I invite him on the rug but suggest his cereal stay out. I have brought cookies, and I invite him to share some with me. He's thrilled. We begin in our normal way and he chooses the picture of Jesus with the girl.

BRANDAN. I need all these. (*Dumps all the rocks outside of the bag and begins to arrange them. I think he is bored with this listening tool.*)

LACY. Can you point out three rocks that tell a story about you and God? (*Brandan begins to stack the rocks but doesn't respond to my question.*) How about a time today when you've been happy or sad? (*Again, nothing.*) Would you like to tell me what happened at the Boys and Girls Club? (*Brandan looks me in the eye and says no. I respect his boundary and make space for him to stack rocks until he becomes restless.*) How about this? Would you like to play with this while I tell you a story?

BRANDAN. Yeah. What is it? Oh, there is a boat and these people. Are the big people like you and the little people, like me? Oh, and I get it; it's like water—like a lake. Oh, this guy is bendy. Okay. I can play with them? What's this, like a carpet or something?

LACY. Can I tell you the story, and we can play with these?

BRANDAN. Yes!

(*Quietly and slowly I tell him the story of Jesus and his friends on a boat in a lake. Jesus is so tired that he takes a nap. While he is sleeping there is a big storm. To play the big storm we take the edges of the blue felt lake and shake it, creating the waves and the unsteadiness of the boat and its people. Then I say that Jesus' friends are afraid, and they wake him up and tell him that they are afraid. Jesus then stands and says "Peace. Be still" to the water, and the water does just what he said. Brandan listens to the story and plays with the people through my telling. He continues but tells his own story.)*

LACY. What are those? (*Brandan has taken the blocks from another set and is putting them in the water.*)

BRANDAN. Sharks. Help me be the storm.

(*Brandan and I shake the blue felt and all the people fall out of the boat and the sharks begin to eat them. Jesus tries to fight them off, but in Brandan's story Jesus is unable to save them. Brandan plays the story again and again. On his last telling of his story, he takes the battery-powered candle and drops it into the scene. The sharks are blown away and Jesus says "thanks very much" to the light.*)

LACY. Is God in this story?

BRANDAN. He's the candle.

LACY. How is he like the candle?

BRANDAN. Can I use the bubbles?

LACY. Okay.

BRANDAN. (*Begins to blow the bubbles. He only says one sentence during his prayer time.*) I love you, and your brother is gone. (*Looks at me, instead of the bubbles.*)

LACY. I'm sorry.

BRANDAN. I'm mad about that.

LACY. Can you tell God that you are mad?

BRANDAN. I did. (*Plays with the bubbles for a few more minutes and then I invite him into blessing because our time is up.*) Do this with the blessing balm and this. (*Picks up a washable marker.*)

LACY. Okay. One on each hand?

BRANDAN. Yeah. That's good!

LACY. Brandan, God loves you very much. God is always with you. God will never leave you. (*I say this twice. Once with each hand.*)

Brandan didn't mention his brother until the prayer time. I wonder if this is a pain he feels he can only tell to God. I mourn for the peace he barely knows.

Session 4. Brandan was excited to be here because he missed last week. We began in our normal way with prayer. When I finished, he said he didn't want to do the rocks; instead, he wanted to play with the "Jesus and the boat." And so we began.

LACY. Can I tell the story of Jesus and his friends in the boat?

BRANDAN. Okay.

(*As I told the story, I wondered if he was listening. He was submerged into his world with Jesus and his friends in the boat on the water. He spent several minutes setting the pieces up perfectly.*)

BRANDAN. How about this?

LACY. Looks good to me. You can move them around. You can play with them.

BRANDAN. Yeah, I know. But I don't want to mess them up. I don't want them to move.

LACY. Why don't you want them to move?

BRANDAN. (*Shrugs his shoulders.*) They're perfect.

LACY. Which one is you?

BRANDAN. This one. (*Points to one of the people. Then he begins to play. He shakes the blue felt and the people fall out of the boat. The shark tries to eat them, but the battery-powered light comes to the rescue and stabs and then roasts the shark.*) We're having roast shark for dinner.

(*We both laugh. Soon afterward Brandan loses interest in the set.*)

LACY. Would you like to make a prayer tool you can take with you?

BRANDAN. I like the beads. Is it like the beads?

LACY. It is, a bit.

(*I take out a box of beads and invite him to choose a colored cross. He does. We have some trouble threading the cord through the hole in the cross.*)

LACY. God, will you help us get this?

(*As we are working together, we have a conversation about prayer and God.*)

LACY. Sometimes, God uses our hands to help others. Like he is using our hands together to get this cord through the hole.

BRANDAN. My hands?

LACY. Yes. How has God used your hands to help?

BRANDAN. I like to help. I help with the dishes, and I help Miss Heather. Yeah. Let's ask God. God, will you help us? (*We don't get the cord through the hole, so we choose a different cord that is thinner.*)

This cord helped us too. (*Picks up the new, smaller cord.*)

LACY. Yes. I think so. (*We finally get the cross threaded, and now we can choose beads.*) Choose three beads that remind you of God.

BRANDAN. (*Chooses three red hearts.*) These beads remind me of God because he loves everyone. (*He and I have to work together to thread the beads.*) He's using our hands again.

LACY. Yes, he is. Now choose three beads that remind you that God wants to talk with you. (*Brandan chooses two clear beads and one that is sparkly.*) Tell me about these beads.

BRANDAN. You can see through them, and they are sparkly. I ask God, "Will you bring my brother home?" And it's been two years, and I miss him. And I ask and he says, "Nope not yet." I'm sad again. (*I wonder what parts of this story are shaped by what he's heard from others.*)

LACY. I'm sorry that you miss your brother.

BRANDAN. (*Uses the beads to pray.*) God, I want my brother. I miss him, and I'm sad and mad. (*Says this while moving his fingers along his prayer beads. When he finishes he looks up at me.*) Can you give me a blessing?

LACY. Sure. Would you like the blessing balm?

BRANDAN. Yeah, but I will bless you.

LACY. Okay. What if we bless each other?

BRANDAN. Okay.

(*I bless him first, and then he blesses me. The understatement of the year.*)

Honestly, I found myself restless when he was playing. I wanted him to find some meaning or to use the pieces in the way I thought they ought to be used. I am continually learning to lean into the space where the Spirit is directing, trusting the Father for this little one and resisting the urge to set him straight.

The listening adult will have to surrender the need to control the prayer space. Our adult notions of what prayer looks like and sounds like can get in the way of us being present with a child in prayer. A child's honest and authentic prayer may challenge our taboos about prayer. It is important to notice when this happens in us and talk about it with a trusted friend or spiritual director. During prayer, children will naturally lean into the Spirit. The longing to connect is so strong in them that it doesn't need pushing. Children come with desire, which is the only condition God requires. The role of the listening adult is to provide space, a few prayer tools, and acceptance.

Acceptance does not mean that we approve of all the child's behavior.[5] There are boundaries in spiritual conversation. Boundaries are life-giving limits that cultivate honor. For example, I would never allow a child to break the items we use. While there may be times when a child wants to break things, I invite them to express their strong emotions in a way that honors the next child that may want to use the items. I would also never allow a child to hit or harm me. Holding this boundary allows a child to honor me. Adult listeners also honor a child's boundary by keeping appropriate physical contact with the child. This means that a spiritual director does not instigate appropriate physical contact without the child's consent. Appropriate physical contact looks like touching a child's hand when offering the blessing balm at the end of the session and perhaps a hug at the beginning or the ending of the session, but only if a child requests a hug. In this way we speak honor to the child. We say that your body is yours and not mine, and you get to say what you'd like to do with it.

Spiritual conversations with children are experiential in nature. The child's whole self is involved. In his book on the Holy Spirit, John Oliver reminds us "humans are better suited to experience God than to explain Him."[6] Prayer for children is an experience of connecting with God. They will experience God not only with their minds (thoughts and feelings) but also with their bodies, their will (their ability to choose), and their relationships with others.

SOAKING IT IN

The following are suggested topics for conversation with God, with others, or even with yourself.

- As you think about the dimensions of the whole person: mind (thoughts and emotions), body, will, and social context, which dimensions do you primarily engage as you connect with God? Are you primarily a mind or social context person? Are you a body person?

- Engage Luke 2:41-52 with your imagination. What do you think it was like for Jesus to be a boy? As you read this passage does any memory from your own childhood come to mind?

- Reflect on your own taboos about prayer. What do you feel is necessary in prayer? What do you feel is off limits? Engage in a listening conversation with God about what surfaces.

- Change your prayer practices. Connect with God using a practice that engages your body or your social context. Notice what new ways open up for connection with God.

- Think back to creating the finger labyrinth: What was the most difficult part about it? What do you sense is the Spirit's invitation in the difficulty?

eight

TWO FRIENDS ON
AN EXPEDITION

*Children who apperceive spiritual experience need adults who can
demonstrate the capacity to listen, and to take them seriously.*

BRENDEN HYDE

E RIC AND I HAD BEEN MEETING before the school day started
for spiritual conversations. We began meeting after reading *Ordinary
Miracles* by Stephanie S. Tolan. This book about life, death, faith, and
doubt gave words to questions and wonderings that had been
stirring in Eric's heart and mind. His mother asked if I would meet
with him. Eric entered our spiritual conversations with all the curiosity, wonder, and awe of his fourth-grade self. He brought his real
questions about his parents' divorce, his great love of and proclivity
for rap music, and his inklings that there was something more to be
experienced than what could be seen. The end of the school year
was upon us, and it meant that our time would be coming to a close.

To mark how God had been present in the last six months, Eric
wandered through his memories naming all the ways and places he

had experienced God. He included what he had learned about his new Friend and some of the good times they shared. There was no secular or sacred in Eric's spirituality. His list included the new bike he got for his birthday, fun times with his brother, his sense of God's presence when his hamster died, and Sunday morning worship when he got to share the rap he composed.

With colorful markers, Eric wrote words and phrases from each remembrance on "fancy paper" that I provided. "Maybe I'll turn them into rap," he said as he wrote. The last thing Eric added was my name. It was a humbling moment. I hadn't really *done* much. Eric had enough "doers" in his life; what he needed was a listener with an open heart. He needed an adult who could come alongside him without judgment, one who could ask the questions his heart really wanted to explore. He needed a safe space to intentionally engage love's extravagant invitation.

WHO ARE THESE LISTENING FRIENDS?

In her book *The Sense of Wonder* Rachel Carson seems to understand the posture of the adult who seeks to accompany children on their spiritual journey when she reflects on her walks with a child in nature: "I am sure no amount of drill would have implanted the names (of the flora and fauna) so firmly as just going through the woods in the spirit of two friends on an expedition of exciting discovery."[1] When we accompany children in their life with God, helping them to recognize and respond, we are two friends on an expedition of exciting discovery into the heart of Christ.

A listening friend to a child can be a parent, grandparent, teacher, pastor, or friend who desires to journey with a child in their life with

God. These listening friends are willing to come alongside rather than lead. They are willing to set aside the urge to correct or teach children. As in all of reality, spiritual conversations with children are trinitarian in nature. At all times the listening adult seeks to be aware and attentive to the child and the Spirit. Ignatius of Loyola (who helped to establish the ministry of spiritual direction) offered a guiding principle of letting the "Creator deal with the creature."[2] In essence the posture of the listening adult is a sideline one, ministering at the elbow. At the side of a child we listen, invite, mirror, encourage, and hold mystery.

It may seem obvious, but a listening friend with children gives time and attention to their own inner life. They may have a spiritual director or spiritual friend who walks with them. An adult listener is also working through their own picture of God so they can, with authenticity, reflect the posture of the welcoming, nonanxious presence of the Community of Love.

A listening friend to children will be an ongoing learner in the ways of the Spirit, always learning to see and hear more clearly the movement of the Spirit in a child's everyday living. An adult who listens with children is willing to engage spiritual conversation whenever the child is ready, whether those conversations happen at bedtime, in the car, over a meal, on a walk, in church, at the grocery store, in play, or in a more formal listening session. Listening adults honor the unbelievable gift of will each child has been given. They honor choice and the invitation offered multiple times over the course of each day to turn and respond to God's bid for connection or to turn away from the bid.

A listening friend is able to not only keep a child's confidences but also the child's safety by sharing with authorities when a child has been harmed or is in danger. The friend will learn to recognize the movement of God in the life of a child and be able to make space for that child to respond to God's movement. Listening friends are ongoing learners in the various ways that all the dimensions of a person are invited to connect with God. They ask more questions and make fewer statements. They embody a centered, steady, welcoming curiosity for the child before them. Silence is a grace in their presence. Being flexible people of prayer, they can pray with bubbles, with paint, with bodies, with sand, with breath, or with nothing at all.

In sacred conversations, listeners create the space and then, as much as they are able, get out of the way. The unseen Person in the room is listening, speaking, and interacting, and listeners know they are witnessing the sacred. It is true that a listening posture can be initially disorienting to the adult who has been in a leadership role with children. Listeners with children never force, coerce, or condemn a childhood experience because it may not be fully understood by the adult. Instead, the child and the experiences are held tenderheartedly and nurtured through thoughtful listening and curious questions.

A listening friend is a person of blessing. The friend's own life radiates confidence in the generosity of Love's Family. The blessedness that the friend knows isn't the stuff of bumper stickers and babble but is a sincere and solid knowledge that God is near in every aspect of a child's life. Blessing flows from the deep well within them that knows every child was created from connection and for connection.

LISTENING FRIEND IN SCRIPTURE

Spiritual conversations with children are not a product of modernity or a new way of being with children. Children and their listening friends have embarked on expeditions with God throughout human history. A helpful example is found in 1 Samuel 3:1-10. In this well-known passage God speaks to Samuel, and Eli gets to accompany him. As we wander through this passage, notice the expedition Samuel seems to be on, and notice how his adult listening partner, Eli, stays at the elbow.

The boy Samuel was ministering to the LORD under Eli. The word of the LORD was rare in those days; visions were not widespread. (I wonder if there was something about a child's way of being that made it possible for this child to hear God.)

At that time Eli, whose eyesight had begun to grow dim so that he could not see, (I wonder in what ways my age and weariness with the world keep me from seeing or hearing God.) was lying down in his room; the lamp of God had not yet gone out, and Samuel was lying down in the temple of the LORD, where the ark of God was. (I wonder why this child is sleeping next to the ark of God. What inside of Samuel drew him to this space? Can we get a bit of the shape of his desire for God? What in him reflected God's longing for connection?)

Then the LORD called, "Samuel! Samuel!" and he said, "Here I am!" and ran to Eli, and said, "Here I am, for you called me." (I wonder about proximity. How can we be near enough to children to be of help, but out of the way enough that they can hear God themselves?) But he said, "I did not call; lie

135

down again." (Eli offered an honest mirror. He didn't try to solve the mystery—perhaps because he didn't know—he was simply a mirror. Or maybe he is just blooming tired!) So he went and lay down. The LORD called again, "Samuel!" (I wonder in what ways we can learn to trust that when the God of the universe wants to be heard and there is a willing listener God will not give up. God will keep calling and calling.) Samuel got up and went to Eli, and said, "Here I am, for you called me." Then Eli perceived that the LORD was calling the boy. (Eli is in formation. I am in formation. I wonder how to hold my own discernment with a gentle hand. Noting when I have missed the voice of the Lord and sensing the grace to listen again.) Therefore Eli said to Samuel, "Go, lie down; and if he calls you, you shall say, 'Speak LORD, for your servant is listening.'" (I wonder how Eli knew to offer Samuel this simple direction but to stay out of the way. I wonder if he wanted to listen in. I wonder if Eli longed for the days when he heard God in that way.) So Samuel went and lay down in his place. (I wonder how Samuel's own longing for God moved him to both sleep near the ark and now to go back one more time and listen, ready to respond.)

Now the LORD came and stood there, calling as before, "Samuel, Samuel!" And Samuel said, "Speak, for your servant is listening." (I wonder what it was like for Samuel to experience his own longing to connect with this God who answered in person. Was he afraid, joyful, peaceful? What kind of courage did it take to say, "Speak, for your servant is listening"?)

Which of my wonderings were your wonderings too? What did you notice about Samuel and Eli's brief conversation? What did you notice about the conversation between Samuel and the Lord? Take a moment to write what you noticed. Begin a conversation with God about these wonderings.

I noticed that Samuel actually *had* a listening friend. While it is clear that the Lord spoke directly to Samuel, Samuel needed someone who would be near enough and safe enough to help him recognize and respond to God. For centuries Christian adults have had formal listening relationships found outside of friendship and family. These ministers are called spiritual directors, and they are formed specifically for the purpose of accompanying others in their life with God.

Imagine what it would look like to value a child's life with God with such weight that spiritual directors, who are already trained to accompany adults in their life with God, could be trained to accompany children in the distinct way they are created? Imagine pastors and teachers learning to attend the inner life of a child. It might look something like what happens at Haven House.

TWO FRIENDS LISTENING AT HAVEN HOUSE

At Haven House I meet with children in the playroom. It is filled with donated stuff. Crawling up the sides of the walls are mounds of discarded plastic toys, some of which are broken. This room is not unlike the lives of the children I sit with; they are bursting with discarded distractions and the shock of early wounding. It can be hard to hear the voice of God through pain, loss, and loneliness. In an attempt to heighten our awareness of the sacred in the midst of a sea of ordinariness, I mark our space with a white fleece blanket dotted with green leaves. My weekly ritual consists of carefully stacking the toys up the sides of the walls and making sure all their buttons are switched off. Last, I center the blanket in the middle of the room as an act of hope: hope that God will meet each child in their need, hope that goodness and beauty still exist in lives marked by tumult.

Because the room was once a dorm room for residents, there is a door with no window. In order to honor the safety of the child, we must have a window. This is a nonnegotiable aspect of meeting with children. When we began meeting with children at Haven House, this was our first obstacle. However, it was easily met by drawing from my familial proclivity to Southern engineer. I took several yards of canvas, a bit of clear plastic vinyl, a curtain rod, a few removable hooks, and created a hanging-curtain door of sorts. Now we have the privacy and safety we need.

When we, the child and myself, enter the room together, we take off our shoes, a signal to the body that we are entering a different time in the midst of ordinary space. As we sit on the blanket together, I invite the child to turn on our battery-powered candle. In this action we remember that God is with us. I had the privilege of meeting with a five-year-old child with Down syndrome for a season. Each time she came, we would take off our shoes, sit down, and engage for about five minutes (which often seemed like an eternity; certainly I have in some ways lost what G. K. Chesterton calls "the infancy of the Father") in the prayer practice of turning on the candle.[3] She would hold the candle with an awesome reverence and tap the flame gently while saying, "God loves me, and God loves you."

This ritual was entirely of her own making on our first meeting. After her prayer proclamations, she would say, "Your turn." And I would do the same, mirroring her movements and her words. "God loves me, and God loves you." The practice was not complete until we had gone through four or five rhythms. I wonder how God was working in those words and movements. I could certainly sense God's presence, but the details of what was actually happening still elude me.

Most children, however, simply turn on the candle and place it next to a mini easel. After that, I ask the child if I can pray for our time together. The prayer is very simple, something like, "Thank you for Josie. Would you help me to listen well to Josie and help Josie to listen well to you? Amen." When I ask children if I can pray to begin our session, they nod or offer some form of affirmation, even when they have had little exposure to God or religious expressions. However, about six months into my first year meeting with children, I had one child who, when asked, vehemently rejected any such notion of prayer. "Okay. Not a problem," I said. "We don't have to pray. Instead, could we close our eyes and imagine something good or beautiful?"

He agreed and we did just that for about a minute. As I opened my eyes and began to get out the holy listening stones, he said, "Don't you want to know why I don't pray?" The truth is I wanted to ask at that very moment, but as the tender soul of a child is like a wild animal, I assumed that this one was already spooked. I didn't want to pry and scare him, but I did want to know. "If you would like to tell me, I'd like to listen," I said, draining as much eagerness from my voice as I could. In the next ten or so minutes this precious child of God unloaded a torrent of fury.

He told the story of how he and his mother had arrived at Haven House having nowhere else to go as they fled from his abusive dad. The church had been a source of strength and comfort for them before they left, but after leaving no one helped. The church only told her to go back to her husband. All the murky details surrounding this horrible family situation were reduced to one angry conclusion, "We needed God, and God wasn't there." Inwardly, I agreed with him. A god who rejects an abused woman and her son isn't a god I want to know or talk with either. This child taught me a valuable lesson.

Making assumptions about a child's experience of God or religious traditions limits the sharing. I learned to create a wider space so that the child could do the leading. Instead, in our sessions we attended to what was good, beautiful, and true in his life. We noticed the kindness of others and named and released some of his pain. He was only at Haven House for three weeks, and then he was gone. Three meetings and never a mention of God, but God certainly *was* there. In the listening, tears, and tender moments God heard and acknowledged his pain and anger.

Next, we move into the projection of desires and longing onto the "Jesus and Me" images. The invitation is extended to choose one of the images and to place it on the mini easel.[4] With the candle and the image we are beginning to build an altar in our sacred space. Some children do not know who Jesus is. When I ask the child to tell me a bit about the image, I ask who they see. If they don't name the stereotypical Jesus-looking figure as Jesus or God, which some do, I have a sense that they may not have a traditionally Christian understanding of the divine. The longing and desires conveyed in the image are still there, and they do offer a glimpse of the interior life of the child, but it's a clue for me to widen my listening. I am aware that the Spirit is present and active, listening to this child even when they do not know who Jesus is.

Depending on desires of the child and the movement of the Spirit, we might use the holy listening stones to begin to recognize the movement of the Spirit, or we might play out a story of Jesus using other materials. Both of these experiences are invitations for the child to their life. It is a great and sacred honor to listen to children in this way. And as such we never *pretend* to know more than we do, we never *push* the child to share more than they are ready to share, and we never *presume* to know what God is doing in the life of a child. Dallas Willard calls these the three *P*s of humility. Humility is the life-giving posture of listening with children.

As children share their lives and their experiences of God, the adult is listening for a moment when vulnerability and invitation intersect. We may sense the opportunity to help the child unpack or savor their experience of God. I think of it more like a *thin space*, a phrase Celtic Christians use to convey the space where heaven and earth come together, or a moment that shines just a little bit brighter, a moment that has a little more heat, as all moments are authentic to the child or they wouldn't share them with us. The moment often looks like recognizing one of the pings.[5] A moment where goodness, beauty, or truth is evident or a moment when wonder, awe, tears, or mystery is shared. It is important to note that the simple act of active listening to another is a ping in itself. In the sharing of their story the child is offering us to connect with them. When we actively listen, we answer that invitation with an affirmation and therefore become one of the ways that the child experiences God. After we have explored or savored the ping, we move into the act of responding to love's invitation.

At the conclusion of our time together a blessing is almost always offered and given. In a stroke of pure genius, chaplain to children LeAnn Hadley came up with the idea of blessing balm.[6] Blessing balm is essentially a tube of clear or opaque lip balm with a new label in place of the old one marking it "Blessing Balm." I like to use eucalyptus-scented lip balm. At the conclusion of our first meeting I explain that while this really and truly is only a tube of lip balm, it can be a reminder of God or of goodness or beauty. Drawing a Celtic cross (because a Celtic cross simply gets more goo on the hand) on the back of the child's hand I say, "Like God (or goodness or beauty) can be hard to see, we can sometimes get a glimmer or catch the scent of God. This is just a reminder to keep an eye or an ear out for God." The children love to be blessed! I usually say something like this, "(the child's name), God loves you very much, and God is always near. Keep looking and listening and talking with God." Or something like, "Goodness and beauty are all around you. Keep looking and listening and watching."

This is what accompanying children looks like at Haven House, but it certainly is not the only way to accompany children. Parents, grandparents, pastors, and teachers also are called to accompany the children in their midst. When children have a listening companion who hears, acknowledges, and encourages their early experiences with God, these experiences take root and blossom into a lifelong relationship.

SOAKING IT IN

The following are suggested topics for conversation with God, with others or even with yourself.

- Reread 1 Samuel 3:1-10. Revisit your wonderings in this passage. Notice which wondering has some energy around it. Engage in a conversation with God about that wondering.

- Reflect on how your own life with God has been an expedition into the heart of Christ. What have you discovered in this season of your expedition?

- How has your picture of God changed since you were a child?

- Reflect on spiritual direction as a ministry at "the elbow." What has been your typical relationship with children, and how might this new posture challenge you?

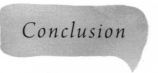

MYSTERY

The indwelling of Christ is a thought particularly fit for the
children, because their large faith does not stumble at the mystery,
their imagination leaps readily to the marvel, that the
King Himself should inhabit a little child's heart.

CHARLOTTE MASON

Aᴼᴼᴛᴇʀ ᴇɪɢʜᴛ ᴄʜᴀᴘᴛᴇʀs ᴏꜰ ᴇxᴘʟᴏʀɪɴɢ spiritual conversations with children, I must admit that what happens in the heart of a child is a mystery. This mystery is both a huge relief and a frustrating challenge to adults who want to engage with children. This reality reminds me of my finitude and vulnerability; it challenges and stretches my trust in God. Instead of trusting in my own knowledge, wisdom, and insight, I am invited to trust that the unseen One is an active partner. A child needs a witness to the action, not an instigator. To be a witness is to be alert and noticing; it is to describe what is seen. Witnesses don't produce outcomes or follow formulas. Witnesses tune their ears and eyes and offer their voices as observation and encouragement. A child's spiritual life is gloriously diverse and complex, and as such accompanying a child in their life with God is more art than science.

Pastor and writer George MacDonald offers guidance: "A parent (or adult) must respect the spiritual person of his child, and approach it with reverence, for that too looks the Father in the face and has an audience with Him into which no earthly parent (or adult) can enter even he dared to desire it."[1] At the heart of spiritual conversations with children is the trinitarian Community of Love, who has longed children into existence for the purpose of deep and lasting relationship. This is the mystery we are invited to witness.

The children at Haven House often come from unchurched homes. Most of the language and knowledge they have about God originates from what they have seen on television. However, many children can recall a personal experience that runs counter to pop-culture associations with God. Honestly, I can't explain how this happens; I can only be a witness to it. But perhaps Hans Urs von Balthasar understands the mystery better than I. He says,

> Love is understood to be the most pristine source of all. This understanding opens up in the child the dormant bud of self-awareness. The love between a thou and an I inaugurates the reality of a world which is deeper than simple being because of its absolute boundlessness and plentitude.[2]

The love and longing, which birthed each child into existence, is also present in spiritual conversations and opens the child not only to their own realities but also to the reality of God. The encounter between the child "thou" and the divine "I" opens the child to the enduring actuality that they are not alone.

During a play-filled session of spiritual direction, Bradley told the story of the night his dad was arrested. Bradley was afraid, confused, and hiding when the police entered their tiny apartment and hand-cuffed his dad. As Bradley recalled, in the midst of the screaming, "God's Mom" peeked her head around the corner and suddenly Bradley felt safe. While I have been born and raised Protestant and have little theology of Mary, I know the fingerprints of God. For children who cannot turn to a God who seems male, due to abusive males in their lives, Mary is safe and nurturing. God knows our pain and steps into it to speak in a language we can hear.

I asked a few questions, and Bradley reflected on his experience. He came to the conclusion that God loved him so much that God sent God's very own mother to protect him. At that point Bradley was invited to paint a prayer about this experience. God was present and guiding; Bradley's life was the tool that was used; the life of Jesus, mirrored in Mary, resulted in the desire to be nearer to this God who protects. As a listening adult with children, it is my work to listen for these movements of God.

Adult listeners give these moments voice and provide a safe place for children to reflect. In those times the light of the Trinity, who longs to be in an ever-deepening relationship with children, shines. I cannot define the experience or direct the experience; all I can do is hold the experience with wide-eyed wonder and vulnerability. Mystery is to be experienced, not mangled. It is pure grace. It cannot be planned, programed, or prescribed.

There is spiritual-formation significance to a child growing an in-timate relationship with God. I have witnessed that living out this relationship can take the shape of intentional kindness to others. It can increase resiliency through deepening emotional intelligence and social awareness. These skills create personal steadiness during the twists and turns of life, and stability in the face of uncertainty. They can lead to forgiveness and bravery, baptism, increased hope and freedom, decreased fear and shame, and most especially a greater sense of being with God in the world.

It is my hope that as you have read and engaged with the ideas, practices, and people of this book, you have felt an invitation stir in you. The invitation might feel like your own child self being invited into your adult life, living into the process of becoming whole and centered in the awareness of God's longing and love for you. It might foster renewed attention to the inner lives of the children who live in your house. It might cultivate intentional listening with your grand-children, getting a glimpse of who they are on the inside. It might take the form of revisioning the way your house of worship engages with children. It might mean incorporating spiritual direction with children into your counseling or spiritual direction practice or even developing a spiritual direction with children ministry.

In the end this is my hope and prayer for you:

May you experience children with a renewed heart.

May you become increasingly aware of children and greet them in common places like the grocery store and the park.

May your deepening sensitivity to childhood experiences change the way you think and live.

May you encourage a child's life with God through listening to what is being spoken and also to what is being said.

May your life become one of prayer for children as people who are on the margins of society.

May you honor the God-given autonomy of children, taking special care not to manipulate or smother them.

May you be granted the awe-inspiring opportunity to witness a child's life with God.

ACKNOWLEDGMENTS

Anyone who has ever written, even if only a school essay, knows that writing is a lonely endeavor. Dreaming, researching, reflecting, crafting, and editing are all done in isolation. While this is true at the desk, it is not true in the realm where spirit touches Spirit. Dorothy Day said, "We have all known the long loneliness and we have learned that the only solution is love and that love comes with community."[1] I am deeply grateful for the communities of love I belong to.

My intergenerational small group has been a steady stream of light and encouragement for six years. Thank you, Tamara and Kaiser Liebenthal; Jenn and Emmett Parish; Anne Barger; Phil and Carol Harrold; Julie, Chad, Emily, and William Huffman; Matt and Allyson Cotham; and Doug, Aidan, and Anwen Borgo. Your love, reassurance, laughter, food, prayer, and steadfast presence have eased the burden and nourished my soul. Thank you also to my Renovaré community. You believed in me long before I believed in me, and you prayed to prove it. Thank you to my father and mother, Glenn and Jody Finn, who modeled what transformation and great love look like. And to my brother, Brandan. Your hard-fought faith has fueled mine.

width:995px; height:1491px;

Thank you also to Trevor Hudson, Gary Moon, Ross Tatum, Dee Jaquet, and Cheri Howard. Your encouragement is a grace of kindness. Last, I want to thank Jean and Dave Nevills and Lynn Clouser Holt. Thank you for taking my green, scrappy, and wandering self under your wings. Your guidance and love have shaped and formed me. Certainly, you are smokin' what you're sellin'. Thank you for being wise and faithful friends. I can't believe my holy luck.

Appendix 1

CHILDLIKE VERSION OF PSALM 23

God is my shepherd.

I am a sheep.

The Shepherd makes sure I have everything I need.

The Shepherd leads me to safe pastures where I can lie down
    and rest.

The Shepherd leads me to green pastures where I can find
    grass to eat.

The Shepherd leads me to pools of water where I can drink.

The Shepherd heals all the parts of me that are broken or hurt.

Sometimes we walk through a dark valley, sometimes a
    death valley.

But I am not afraid, because the Shepherd is with me.

The Shepherd walks next to me.

The Shepherd's trusty crook makes me feel safe.

You, Good Shepherd, will take care of me even when I am
    surrounded by enemies.

You, Good Shepherd, give me food, good food.

You, Good Shepherd, still choose me and like me, when no
    one else does.
I am surrounded by good. I am surrounded by kindness.
You are my home Good Shepherd; I live in you and you
    live in me.
Forever.

Worship Woodworks (worshipwoodworks.com) has sets of wooden materials
and figures on Psalm 23 as well as sets on the life of Jesus.

Appendix 2

THREE GUIDED PRAYER
PAGES FOR WALKING
A LABYRINTH

WALKING WITH JESUS

Remove your shoes.

Take a deep breath; see if you can breathe in all the way to your toes.

One more.

And one more.

Begin to walk slowly.

See if you can feel each part of your foot on the path.

First your heel, then the middle part of your foot, then the ball of your foot, then your toes.

Do this for a few steps.

What part of your body feels heavy today?

Talk with Jesus about that.

Was there a time today you felt afraid? Talk with Jesus about that.

Was there a time today you felt lonely? Talk with Jesus about that.

When you arrive at the center take three deep breaths and talk with Jesus who loves you.

Invite Jesus to walk with you carrying your heaviness.

Begin to walk your way out. Feel each part of your foot touching the labyrinth.

Imagine what it will look like tomorrow when Jesus carries your heaviness.

As you finish thank Jesus for taking a walk with you.

REFLECTING WITH JESUS

Remove your shoes.

Take a deep breath.

One more.

And one more.

Begin to walk slowly.

As you walk, reflect upon your day.

In what ways is this walk like your day?

Choose two things that you are thankful for today. Talk with Jesus about them.

Choose two things that you wish didn't happen today. Talk with Jesus about them.

When you arrive at the center, take three deep breaths and talk with Jesus who loves you.

Invite Jesus to walk with you into tomorrow.

Talk with Jesus about one thing you are looking forward to tomorrow.

Talk with Jesus about one thing you are dreading for tomorrow.

Imagine what it will look like tomorrow when Jesus walks with you in the good and difficult parts.

As you near the end, thank Jesus for taking a walk with you and for walking with you as you leave.

Walking with the Good Shepherd

Remove your shoes.

Take three deep and slow breaths.

Close your eyes and imagine that you are a sheep and that God is a shepherd.

Begin to walk slowly while praying the following prayer as you walk to the center.

God is my Shepherd and I am a sheep.

He makes sure I have everything I need.

He leads me to green pastures where I can lie down and rest.

He leads me to green pastures where I can have grass to eat.

He shows me where there are pools of water so I can drink.

He heals all the parts of me that are broken or hurt.

Sometimes I walk through dark valleys, sometimes through a
       death valley.

But I am not afraid because my Good Shepherd is with me.

He walks next to me.

His trusty shepherd's crook makes me feel safe.

You, Good Shepherd, take care of me even when I am
       surrounded by enemies.

You give me food, good food.

You like me, choose me, when no one else does.

Good is all around me.

Mercy is all around me.

You are my home, Good Shepherd, I live in you and you live
       in me.

Forever.

When you get to the center take three deep breaths. Talk with Jesus about how a sheep feels.

As you walk out of the labyrinth, pray Psalm 23 again. (Read the words of the prayer again.)

As you near the end, thank Jesus for taking a walk with you in your imagination. Invite Jesus to keep talking with you.

Appendix 3

A CHILDLIKE ADAPTATION OF THE LORD'S PRAYER WITH BODIES

SAY: "My Father/Mother who is near me."[1]

Stand erect with your feet shoulder-width apart and arms stretched to the sky.

SAY: "May everyone love your name."

Keep your body in the same position and smile the biggest smile you have toward God.

SAY: "May you continue to make the world whole—just as heaven is whole in you."

Sweep your arms wide, opening up to heaven, then down by your side like you are holding a large basket.

SAY: "Give me today, the things I need for today."

Sit on the floor and open your hands for what you need. Imagine what you need in your hands. Receive it and pour it into your heart or mouth or mind. Do this over and over until you have asked for all you need.

Say: "Forgive me as I am learning to forgive others."

Place one hand on your heart and the other hand open to receive. Think about something that happened this week that made you feel sad or hurt. Talk to God about it. When you have finished, wrap both arms around yourself in a big hug.

Say: "Rescue me from trials and anything bad."

From the sitting position come up to your knees and place your hands on your waist. Hold in your mind a worry you have. Ask God to help you with it.

Say: "You, God, are in charge. And you have all the power and all the glory—which is just the way I want it."

Stand up and run around grabbing power and glory and strength, and put it in an imaginary basket and then lift the basket up to God.

Say: "Let it be!"

Jump for joy!

Appendix 4

HOLY LISTENING INFORMATION AND PERMISSION FORM

HOLY LISTENING

A ministry in which children are heard and supported as they seek
to make meaning of the experiences of their lives

INFORMATION

Name of Child: _____

_____

Child's Address:_____

_____

Child's Birthday: _____

_____

Name of Parent/Guardian: _____

_____

Address: _____

_____

Primary Phone: _____

2nd Phone: _____

Parent/Guardian Email Address: _____

_____

Describe the child's living situation (household members, etc.):

_____

_____

_____

_____

Faith community affiliation: _____

_____

Have you read and understood the ministry as described in our brochure? (Circle one) YES or NO

Do you understand that by signing this form you agree that the content of the session will be kept confidential (including not revealing content to the parent or guardian), excepting only that information which must be reported by law? (Circle one) YES or NO

By signing below, I give permission for a holy listening provider to meet with my child. I affirm that I have read the informational brochure and understand that the ministry provided is spiritual and not psychological in nature.

(Print Name) _____

_____

(Sign Name) _____

(Date) _____

HOLY LISTENING

A ministry where children are heard and supported as they seek to make meaning of the experiences of their lives

WHAT IS HOLY LISTENING?

- A place where children receive undivided attention as they express themselves about the experiences of their lives.

- A "soul friend," someone who helps children recognize and respond to the presence of God in their lives.

- Confidential. We will never reveal what your child says to anyone unless it is for their own protection (as mandated by law).

- Safe. We observe accepted practices that ensure the child's safety whenever he or she talks with us.

With the Spirit as the true listener and the child as the center of attention, a holy listener becomes a soul friend with whom children can talk and share. A holy listener is present with undivided attention as a witness as a child shares about their experiences. A holy listener also helps the child recognize and respond to the movement of God in every experience. Holy listening may include playing with toys, expression through art, and talking with God using various means.

Each session lasts between thirty and forty-five minutes, depending on the age of the child and the circumstances they face. The child, the parent/guardian, and the holy listener will determine how often to meet. Although confidentiality and safety are of the utmost importance, *holy listening is not counseling, psychotherapy, or a fix-it methodology.* However, if abuse is suspected or the child is a danger to their own selves or others, the holy listener will notify the authorities as required by law.

NOTES

INTRODUCTION: LEARNING FROM CHRISTOPHER

[1]The names of the children and the details of their stories have been changed throughout this work to honor their privacy.

[2]The first six paragraphs of this chapter overlap with an article by Lacy Finn Borgo, "Children's Spirituality: God Makes the First Move," *Renovaré*, accessed July 1, 2019, https://renovare.org/articles/childrens-spirituality-god-makes-the-first-move.

1. LEARNING FROM JESUS

[1]Much of this section is taken from Lacy Finn Borgo, "Help Along the Way: Let's Talk About Talking," *Good Dirt Ministries* (blog), May 3, 2018, www.gooddirt ministries.org/blog/2018/5/3/help-along-the-way-lets-talk-about-talking.

[2]Lisa Miller, *The Spiritual Child: The New Science on Parenting for Health and Lifelong Thriving* (New York: Picador, 2015), 3, Kindle.

[3]Imago Dei Ministries Reflection Cards can be found at www.idmin.org/resources.

2. CHILDREN'S SPIRITUAL FORMATION

[1]Patrick Henry Reardon, "The Man Alive: Irenaeus Did Not Teach Self-Fulfillment," *Touchstone*, October 13-15, 2016, accessed February 21, 2016, www .touchstonemag.com/archives/article.php?id=25-05-003-e.

[2]Dallas Willard, *The Divine Conspiracy: Rediscovering Our Hidden Life in God* (New York: HarperCollins, 1997), loc. 587, Kindle.

[3]Edward Robinson, *The Original Vision* (Oxford: Religious Experience Research Unit, 1977), 15.

3. POSTURE, POWER, AND PATTERNS

[1]"Personal power packages" is a Dallas Willard term used in *Renovation of the Heart* (Colorado Springs: NavPress, 2002) and in his lectures during the Renovaré Institute, Denver cohort.

[2]Brendan Hyde, *Children and Spirituality: Searching for Meaning and Connectedness* (London: Jessica Kingsley, 2008), loc. 1105, Kindle.

[3]David M. Csinos and Ivy Beckwith, *Children's Ministry in the Way of Jesus* (Downers Grove, IL: InterVarsity Press, 2013), loc. 619, Kindle.

[4]Sofia Cavalletti, *The Religious Potential of the Child: Experiencing Scripture and Liturgy with Young Children* (Chicago: Liturgy Training, 1992), 45.

[5]Leanne Hadley, "Simple Directions for Making Holy Listening Stones," *Leanne Hadley* (blog), accessed July 1, 2019, www.leanne-hadley.com/holy-listening.

[6]See appendix 4 for sample release forms.

4. The Gift of Eyes and Ears

[1]C. S. Lewis, *The Weight of Glory* (Grand Rapids: Eerdmans, 1949), 15.

[2]Douglas V. Steere, *On Being Present Where You Are* (Lebanon, PA: Pendle Hill, 1967), 16.

[3]Dallas Willard, *The Divine Conspiracy: Rediscovering Our Hidden Life in God* (New York: Harper, 1998), loc. 4352, Kindle.

[4]Willard, *Divine Conspiracy*, loc. 4352.

[5]Leanne Hadley, "Simple Directions for Making Holy Listening Stones," *Leanne Hadley* (blog), accessed July 1, 2019, www.leanne-hadley.com/holy-listening.

[6]Tobin Hart, *The Secret Spiritual World of Children: The Breakthrough Discovery That Profoundly Alters Our Conventional View of Children's Mystical Experiences* (Novato, CA: New World Library, 2003), locs. 1584, 2984, 3870, Kindle.

[7]Hart, *Secret Spiritual World of Children*.

[8]Jerome Berryman, *Teaching Godly Play: How to Mentor the Spiritual Development of Children* (Denver: Morehouse Education Resources, 2009), 54.

[9]Sofia Cavalletti, *The Religious Potential of the Child: Experiencing Scripture and Liturgy with Young Children* (Chicago: Liturgy Training Publications, 1992), 72.

[10]Berryman, *Teaching Godly Play*, 130.

[11]Cavalletti, *Religious Potential of the Child*, 36.

[12]Johannes Baptist Metz, quoted in Diane Millis, *Conversation: The Sacred Art: Practicing Presence in an Age of Distraction* (Woodstock, VT: SkyLight Paths, 2013), 81.

[13]Garry L. Landreth, *Play Therapy: The Art of the Relationship* (New York: Taylor & Francis, 2012), 73, Kindle.

[14]Landreth, *Play Therapy*, 76.

[15]"The gift of ears" is a phrase that Trevor Hudson uses when talking about listening. He concludes that many of us ask the Spirit for the gift of tongues when we also should be asking for the gift of ears. See Trevor Hudson, *The Holy Spirit Here and Now* (Nashville: Upper Room Books, 2013), 116.

5. The Language of Play and Projection

[1]Garry L. Landreth, *Play Therapy: The Art of the Relationship* (New York: Taylor & Francis, 2012), 14, Kindle.

[2]See appendix 1 for a childhood version of Psalm 23 and source for wooden materials and figures.

[3]Jerome Berryman, *Teaching Godly Play: How to Mentor the Spiritual Development of Children* (Denver: Morehouse Education Resources, 2009), 134-37.

[4]Tobin Hart, *The Secret Spiritual World of Children: The Breakthrough Discovery That Profoundly Alters Our Conventional View of Children's Mystical Experiences* (Novato, CA: New World Library, 2003), loc. 849, Kindle.

[5]Vivienne Mountain, "Four Links Between Child Theology and Children's Spirituality," *International Journal of Children's Spirituality* 16, no. 3 (August 2011): 266.

6. ATTENDING THE SPIRIT

[1]Edward Robinson, *The Original Vision: A Study of the Religious Experience of Children* (Oxford: Religious Experience Research Unit Manchester College, 1977), 145.

[2]John W. Oliver, *Giver of Life: The Holy Spirit in Orthodox Tradition* (Brewster, MA: Paraclete Press, 2011), 53.

[3]Trevor Hudson, *The Holy Spirit Here and Now* (Nashville: Upper Room Books, 2013), 80.

[4]Sofia Cavalletti, *The Religious Potential of the Child: Experiencing Scripture and Liturgy with Young Children* (Chicago: Liturgy Training Publications, 1992), 9.

[5]Karl Rahner, "Ideas for a Theology of Childhood," *Theological Investigations* (London: Cox & Wyman, 1982), 3:33-50.

[6]Thomas N. Hart, *The Art of Christian Listening* (New York: Paulist Press, 1980,) 45.

7. WHOLE PERSON PRAYER

[1]Jerome Berryman, *Teaching Godly Play: How to Mentor the Spiritual Development of Children* (Denver: Morehouse Education Resources, 2009), 54.

[2]For the Lord's Prayer with our bodies, see appendix 3.

[3]Alice Fryling, *Seeking God Together: An Introduction to Group Spiritual Direction* (Downers Grove, IL: InterVarsity Press, 2009), 63.

[4]Lacy Finn Borgo, "The Contemplative Practice of Felting a Finger Labyrinth," *Good Dirt Ministries* (blog), May 26, 2019, www.gooddirtministries.org /blog/2019/5/26/the-contemplative-practice-of-felting-a-finger-labyrinth.

[5]Garry L. Landreth, *Play Therapy: The Art of the Relationship* (New York: Taylor & Francis, 2012), 69, Kindle.

[6]John W. Oliver, *Giver of Life: The Holy Spirit in Orthodox Tradition* (Brewster, MA: Paraclete Press, 2011), 51.

8. TWO FRIENDS ON AN EXPEDITION

[1] Rachel Carson, *The Sense of Wonder: Words and Pictures to Help You Keep Alive Your Child's Inborn Sense of Wonder and Renew Your Own Delight in the Mysteries of Earth, Sea and Sky* (New York: Harper & Row, 1998), 23.

[2] Louis J. Puhl, *The Spiritual Exercises of St. Ignatius* (Chicago: Loyola Press, 1951), 6.

[3] G. K. Chesterton, *Orthodoxy* (Wheaton, IL: Harold Shaw, 2001), 84. "It may not be automatic necessity that makes all daisies alike; it may be that God makes every daisy separately, but has never gotten tired of making them. It may be that He has the eternal appetite of infancy; for we have sinned and grown old, and our Father is younger than we."

[4] Jeannette Fernandez, "JesusandMeArt," Etsy, accessed July 1, 2019, www.etsy .com/shop/JesusandMeArt?ref=search_shop_redirect.

[5] Regarding these pings, see "The Trinitarian Community of Love" in chap. 2.

[6] Leanne Hadley, "Reflections on Being a Hospital Chaplain to Children," First Steps: Stepping Up to Wholeness Conference, First United Methodist Church, Grand Junction, Colorado, May 2013.

CONCLUSION

[1] George MacDonald, *Seaboard Parish* (n.p.: Johannesen Printing, 1868), chap. 23.

[2] Hans Urs von Balthasar, *Until You Become Like This Child* (San Francisco: Ignatius Press, 1988), 17-18.

ACKNOWLEDGMENTS

[1] Dorothy Day, *The Long Loneliness: The Autobiography of the Legendary Catholic Social Activist* (New York: HarperOne, 1997), 286.

APPENDIX 3: A CHILDLIKE ADAPTATION OF THE LORD'S PRAYER WITH BODIES

[1] Although the wording here is my own, my version of this prayer was inspired by Dallas Willard's version found in *The Divine Conspiracy: Rediscovering Our Hidden Life in God* (San Francisco: HarperSanFrancisco, 1998), 269.

RECOMMENDED READING

Csinos, David M., and Ivy Beckwith. *Children's Ministry in the Way of Jesus.* Downers Grove, IL: InterVarsity Press, 2013.

Hart, Tobin. *The Secret Spiritual World of Children.* Novato, CA: New World Library, 2003.

Hay, David, and Rebecca Nye. *The Spirit of the Child.* Rev. ed. London: Fount, 2006.

Hyde, Brendan. *Children and Spirituality: Searching for Meaning and Connectedness.* London: Jessica Kingsley, 2008.

Keating, Noel. *Meditation with Children: A Resource for Teachers and Parents.* Dublin, Ireland: Veritas, 2017.

Nye, Rebecca. *Children's Spirituality: What It Is and Why It Matters.* London: Church House, 2009.

Stairs, Jean. *Listening for the Soul: Pastoral Care and Spiritual Direction.* Minneapolis: Fortress Press, 2000.

Stonehouse, Catherine, and Scottie May. *Listening to Children on the Spiritual Journey: Guidance for Those Who Teach and Nurture.* Grand Rapids: Baker Academic, 2010.

BECOMING OUR TRUE SELVES

The nautilus is one of the sea's oldest creatures. Beginning with a tight center, its remarkable growth pattern can be seen in the ever-enlarging chambers that spiral outward. The nautilus in the IVP Formatio logo symbolizes deep inward work of spiritual formation that begins rooted in our souls and then opens to the world as we experience spiritual transformation. The shell takes on a stunning pearlized appearance as it ages and forms in much the same way as the souls of those who devote themselves to spiritual practice. Formatio books draw on the ancient wisdom of the saints and the early church as well as the rich resources of Scripture, applying tradition to the needs of contemporary life and practice.

Within each of us is a longing to be in God's presence. Formatio books call us into our deepest desires and help us to become our true selves in the light of God's grace.

VISIT

ivpress.com/formatio

to see all of the books in the
line and to sign up for the
IVP Formatio newsletter.